MICROECONOMIC PROBLEMS

Concepts, Cases, and Tests
SECOND EDITION

Companion volumes by Edwin Mansfield

MICROECONOMICS: THEORY AND APPLICATIONS, SECOND EDITION

MICROECONOMICS: SELECTED READINGS, SECOND EDITION

MICROECONOMIC PROBLEMS

Concepts, Cases, and Tests
SECOND EDITION

EDWIN MANSFIELD
University of Pennsylvania

W·W·NORTON & COMPANY·INC·

NEW YORK

Contents

Preface

to the Second Edition

This book of problems, concepts, cases, and tests is designed to be used in courses in intermediate microeconomics. I have prepared this material to be used with my text, *Microeconomics: Theory and Applications*, second edition (New York: Norton, 1975). However, I have developed and organized the material in such a way that it can be used to supplement any intermediate microeconomics textbook.

This second edition contains a number of important new features. First, almost 20 percent of the problems are new. These new problems, like a great many of the old ones, are aimed at giving the student some practice in applying microeconomic concepts to real-world problems. Second, I have added four brief cases that should test the student's skill in using microeconomics. They should also help to kindle the student's interest in the subject. Third, the final chapter, dealing with Public Goods, Benefit-Cost Analysis, and Environmental Protection, is new. In view of the importance of these topics, I think that it is high time that they be included in a book of this sort.

Each chapter is composed of three parts. At the beginning there is a list of key concepts that lie at the heart of the aspect of microeconomics under consideration. Then there is a second part which contains about 20 problems, cases, exercises, and essay questions. These questions vary in difficulty, but in practically all cases no mathematics beyond basic algebra is required. (Those requiring any knowledge of calculus are labeled as advanced.) Finally, there is a third part that contains about 30 completion questions, true-false questions, and multiple-choice questions.

In addition, brief answers are provided at the end of the book for practically all of the questions. Naturally, these answers must be truncated and incomplete, in view of the available space. They should not be viewed as complete answers. However, they should prove useful in indicating to the student how well he answered each of the questions. In a few cases, no answer is provided, because the essay question did not permit any simple summary response.

This book has two purposes. First, it should prove useful to students in mastering the subject of microeconomics. It enables them to work through the key concepts in a systematic way and apply these concepts and principles to various problems, exercises, and simple cases. It also provides them with sets of questions that can be used as a self-test to provide feedback concerning their understanding and difficulties. Second, it should prove useful to instructors in finding areas where students are having some difficulty. The book is designed so that, if some instructors prefer students to hand in the exercises, this can easily be done. The pages are perforated. On the other hand, the book is completely self-contained so that the student can use it on his own, if the instructor deems it preferable.

In preparing this material, I have tried to include a comprehensive set of questions which cover the entire spectrum of topics included in most microeconomics courses. Wherever possible, I have tried to include empirical material, as well as problems and cases that illustrate the power of microeconomic theory in aiding decision-makers in both the private and public sectors of the economy. Thus, there is a blend of theory, on the one hand, with measurement and application, on the other. Judging from the response to my textbook, many instructors agree with me that this blend is the most effective way to teach microeconomic theory at the intermediate level.

Philadelphia, 1974 E. M.

MICROECONOMIC PROBLEMS

Concepts, Cases, and Tests
SECOND EDITION

CHAPTER 1 Introduction to Microeconomics

Key Concepts

Economics

Microeconomics

Macroeconomics

Optimal production decisions

Pricing policy

Optimal resource allocation

Public policy concerning market structure

Human wants

Resources

Labor

Land

Capital

Technology

Tasks performed by
    an economic system

The price system

Models

Model-building

Evaluation of a model

Problems and Essays

1. According to Adam Smith, "Monopoly . . . is a great enemy to good management." What do you think he meant? Do you agree or disagree?

2. In aeronautical engineering, models of an airplane are used to investigate its aerodynamic properties in a wind tunnel. Must such models have seats for passengers? Must they be hollow? What functions must they serve?

3. According to Alfred P. Sloan, who was president of General Motors from 1923 to 1937 and chairman of its board of directors from 1937 to 1956, "The great difference between the industry of today as compared to that of yesterday is what might be referred to as the necessity of the scientific approach, the elimination of operation by hunches."* Indicate how microeconomics plays a role in this more scientific approach to management.

4. What does economics deal with? What is the difference between microeconomics and macroeconomics?

*A. Sloan, *Adventures of a White Collar Worker*, Garden City, N.Y.: Doubleday, 1941.

5. Give several examples of the types of problems that microeconomics helps to solve.

6. Is microeconomics concerned solely with the solution of practical problems? Give examples of questions that are dealt with in microeconomics that do not take the form of practical problems. In what sense is microeconomics like mathematics?

7. Define human wants. What role do human wants play in microeconomics?

8. Define economic resources. What role do economic resources play in microeconomics?

9. Describe the various types of economic resources.

10. Define technology. Is there any difference between science and technology? If so, what is the difference? What role does technology play in microeconomics?

11. Describe the four basic tasks that must be performed by any economic system.

12. How does our system determine the level and composition of output in the society?

13. How does our economic system allocate its resources among competing uses and process these resources to obtain the desired level and composition of output?

14. How does our economic system determine how much in the way of goods and services each member of the society is to receive?

15. How does our economic system provide for an adequate rate of growth of per capita income?

16. What is a model? Can the usefulness of a model be deduced from the realism of its assumptions? Why do economists use models?

17. What considerations must be taken into account in judging or evaluating a model?

18. Are the models contained in this book sufficiently accurate to solve all of the problems faced by governments and firms? Have all of them been tested completely? Are they the best available at this time?

Completion Questions

1. Economics is concerned with the way in which _____ are allocated among alternative uses to satisfy _____.

2. Microeconomics deals with the economic behavior of _____ _____ .

3. Wants _____ from individual to individual and over time for the same person.

4. Resources are used to produce _____ .

5. There are two types of resources: economic and _____ .

6. Resources are often classified as land, labor, and _____ .

7. Technology is directed toward _____ ; science is directed toward _____ _____ .

8. In a free enterprise economy, _____ choose the amount of each good that they want, and _____ act in accord with these decisions.

9. In our system, the income of each individual depends largely on how much he owns of each resource and _____ .

10. A nation's rate of growth of per capita income depends on the rate of growth of its resources and the _____ _____ .

True or False

_____ 1. Microeconomics is helpful in promoting an understanding of the powerful modern tools of managerial decision-making.

_____ 2. The lawyer who argues an antitrust case, and the judge who decides one, must both rely on and use the principles of microeconomics.

_____ 3. Microeconomics is concerned only with solving practical problems.

_____ 4. Economic resources sometimes have a zero price.

_____ 5. There usually is only one way of producing a commodity so it is easy to figure out which way is best.

_____ 6. The price system plays some role, but only a minor one, in allocating resources in a free enterprise economy.

_____ 7. In the acquisition of new weapons, society relies exclusively on the price system.

_____ 8. A model cannot be useful if it simplifies and abstracts from reality.

_____ 9. Models are used by economists, but not physicists.

_____ 10. One reason for using a model is that it may be the cheapest way of getting needed information.

Multiple Choice

1. When applied to public policy issues, microeconomics has generally been used by
   a. Democratic administrations.
   b. Republican administrations.
   c. both parties.
   d. neither party.

2. Microeconomics is concerned with
   a. optimal production decisions.
   b. pricing policy.
   c. optimal resource allocation.
   d. antitrust policy.
   e. all of the above.

3. In a free enterprise economy, profits are
   a. the stick used to eliminate less efficient firms.
   b. the carrot used to reward the proper decisions.
   c. both a and b.
   d. neither a nor b.

4. If a model is to be any good, it must
   a. make assumptions that are exact replicas of reality.
   b. refrain from referring to things that are not directly measurable.
   c. predict phenomena in the real world reasonably well.
   d. all of the above.

5. If a model can predict the price of wheat within a penny a bushel, this model
   a. will never be used.
   b. will always be used.
   c. will probably be used if nothing predicts better.

CHAPTER 2 The Tastes and Preferences
of the Consumer

Key Concepts

Indifference curves
Marginal rate of substitution
Convexity
Utility
Cardinal utility
Ordinal utility
Marginal utility
Budget line
Money income
Equilibrium

Indifference map
Market basket
Revealed preference
Conspicuous consumption
Edgeworth box diagram
Contract curve
Determinants of tastes
Exchange between consumers
Rationality
Advertising and selling expenses

Problems and Essays

1. According to *Business Week*, American wine producers "are encouraged by the whole chang-ing social role of their product."* Specifically, the American consumer has become much more attuned to wine. How does the growing acceptance of wine by American consumers affect their indifference curves between wine and other kinds of alcoholic beverages?

Business Week, February 23, 1974, p. 70.

2. In recent years, great numbers of Americans have traveled to Europe. What effect do you think that this has had on American tastes for wine? How could you test your hypothesis?

3. What are the three basic assumptions that economists make about the nature of consumers' tastes?

4. Draw the indifference curve that includes the following market baskets. Each of these market baskets gives the consumer equal satisfaction.

Market basket	Meat (lbs.)	Potatoes (lbs.)
1	2	8
2	3	7
3	4	6
4	5	5
5	6	4
6	7	3
7	8	2
8	9	1

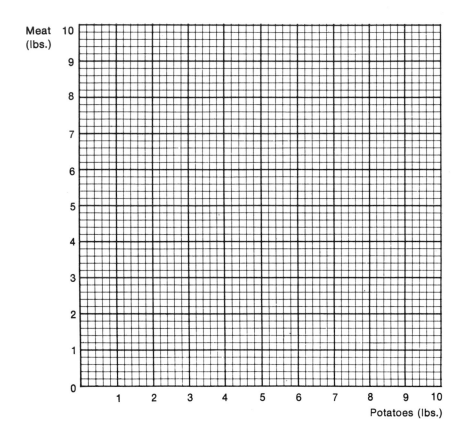

Meat (lbs.)

Potatoes (lbs.)

5. In the previous question, what is the marginal rate of substitution of potatoes for meat? How does the marginal rate of substitution vary as the consumer consumes more meat and less potatoes? Is this realistic?

6. Define utility. How does cardinal utility differ from ordinal utility; Which concept is generally used by economists today?

7. Suppose that the consumer has an income of $10 per period and that he must spend it all on meat or potatoes. If meat is $1 a pound and potatoes are 10 cents a pound, draw the consumer's budget line.

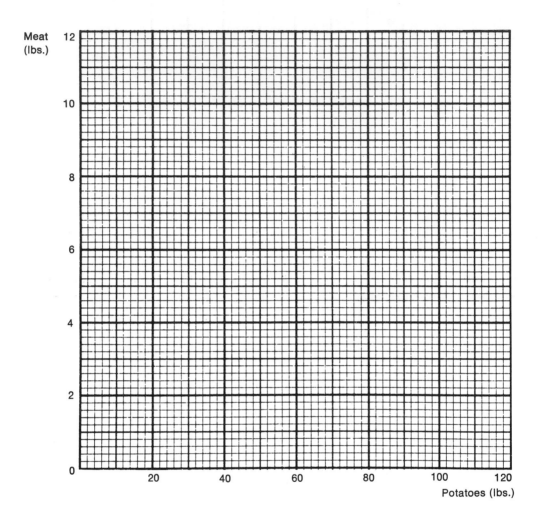

8. In the previous case, what will be the budget line if the consumer's income increases to $12? What will be the budget line if the price of meat increases to $2 per lb.? What will be the budget line if the price of potatoes increases to 20 cents per lb.?

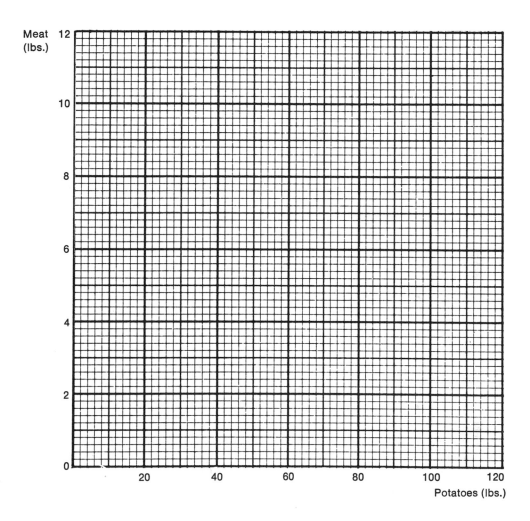

9. What is meant by the theory of revealed preference? Describe how it can be used to measure indifference curves. Is it really a practical measurement technique?

10. What determines consumer tastes and preferences? What is meant by conspicuous consumption?

11. How is an Edgeworth box diagram constructed? What is the contract curve? What practical use does the contract curve have?

12. In the case of the following Edgeworth box diagram, curves 1 and 2 are indifference curves of one consumer, and curves I and II are indifference curves of the second consumer. Is it optimal for the first consumer to receive OX units of good X and OY units of good Y, the second consumer receiving (OC – OX) units of good X and (OB – OY) units of good Y? What allocation would be better?

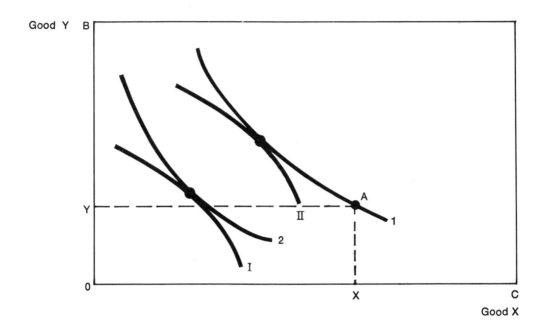

13. (*Advanced*) Suppose Mrs. Brown has $50 to be divided between corn and beans, and that the price of beans is 50 cents per lb. What will be the relationship between the price of corn and the amount of corn she will buy, if her utility function is $U = \log Q_c + 4 \log Q_b$, where U is her utility, Q_c is the quantity of corn she consumes (in lbs.) and Q_b is the quantity of beans she consumes (in lbs.)?

Completion Questions

1. All other things equal, the rational consumer is assumed to prefer _____ of a good to _____ of a good.

2. All market baskets possessing the same utility are said to be on the same _____ _____ curve.

3. The negative of the derivative of the indifference curve is termed the _____ _____ .

4. The rational consumer attempts to _____ his utility subject to a _____ constraint.

5. The condition for consumer equilibrium is that the budget line be _____ _____ an indifference curve.

6. In the Edgeworth box diagram, the locus of points of tangency of the indifference curves of the two consumers is called the _____ curve.

7. If the rational consumer always prefers more of a good to less, it follows that all indifference curves have a _____ slope.

8. If the marginal rate of substitution of good X for good Y at constant utility decreases with the quantity of X, then the indifference curve is _____ .

9. One of the most important determinants of a consumer's behavior is his _____
_____ .

10. The three basic assumptions an economist makes about the nature of consumer tastes are:

If the consumer is presented with two market baskets, he can decide _____
_____ . If the consumer prefers oranges to bananas and bananas to apples, then he

_____ .

The consumer always prefers _____ of a commodity to _____ of it.

11. Different market baskets on the same indifference curve should be given the _____ values of utility.

12. Market baskets on higher indifference curves should receive _____ utilities than market baskets on lower indifference curves.

True or False

_____ 1. Two indifference curves can intersect only when one of the goods being studied is a high-priced item.

_____ 2. Economists generally assume that indifference curves always lie above their tangents.

_____ 3. Indifference curves are always concave to the origin.

_____ 4. The marginal rate of substitution of good X for good Y is the number of units of good X that a customer will accept instead of good Y to increase his satisfaction.

_____ 5. Utility theory assumes that market baskets on higher indifference curves have higher utilities.

_____ 6. Any numbers can be attached to a set of market baskets to represent utility so long as market baskets higher up on the same indifference curve have higher values.

_____ 7. If a consumer's income rises, he will probably buy the same amount of a good.

_____ 8. The shape of a consumer's indifference curve is generally assumed to be unaffected by price changes.

_____ 9. If consumers are on the contract curve, one point on the contract curve is as good as another, as far as they are concerned.

_____ 10. A person's tastes are like his fingerprints: They don't change.

Multiple Choice

1. If point B lies above and to the right of point A on a two-commodity indifference map, and the indifference curve passing through point A is characterized by a utility level of 1, then the utility level of the indifference curve passing through point B has utility:
   a. greater than one.
   b. equal to one.
   c. less than one.

2. Modern microeconomic theory generally regards utility as
   a. cardinal.
   b. ordinal.
   c. independent.
   d. Republican.
   c. Democrat.

3. The consumer is likely to find the market basket that maximizes his utility
   a. immediately.
   b. if time is allowed for him to adapt and learn.
   c. never.

4. The theory of revealed preference is
   a. a practical technique to measure indifference curves.
   b. a useless and discredited version of utility theory.
   c. a means of demonstrating how indifference curves can, in principle, be determined.

5. A basic assumption of the theory of consumer choice is that
   a. the consumer tries to get on the highest indifference curve.
   b. the consumer tries to get the most of good Y.
   c. the budget line is concave.

CHAPTER 3 Consumer Behavior and Individual Demand

Key Concepts

Engel curves
Income-consumption curves
Price-consumption curves
Individual demand curves
Price elasticity of demand
Price-consumption curve
Substitution effect
Income effect
Normal goods

Inferior goods
Real income
Giffen's paradox
Consumers' surplus
Cost of living
Laspeyres index
Paasche index
Index numbers
Unitary elasticity

Problems and Essays

1. According to Karl Fox, "An increase of 10 percent in the farm price of the 'average' food product would be associated with something like a 4 percent increase in the retail price and perhaps a 2 percent decrease in per capita consumption."* Is the price elasticity of demand different at the farm level than at the retail level? Why?

*K. Fox, "Commercial Agriculture," Committee for Economic Development, November 1962, p. 66.

2. James B. Hendry has pointed out, in connection with the demand for fuel, that "Fuel-burning equipment tends to be specialized and costly, and changeovers are generally not made frequently."* What are the implications of this fact for a household's demand for fuel?

3. Show why, if the consumer is to be in equilibrium, the marginal rate of substitution of good X for good Y must equal the ratio of the price of good X to the price of good Y.

*J. B. Hendry, "The Bituminous Coal Industry," in W. Adams, *The Structure of American Industry*, New York: Macmillan, 1961, p. 98.

4. Suppose the following relationship exists between a consumer's income and the amount of eggs he consumes:

Income ($ per week)	Eggs (no. per week)
100	12
150	24
200	36
250	42
300	48

Graph the consumer's Engel curve for eggs below:

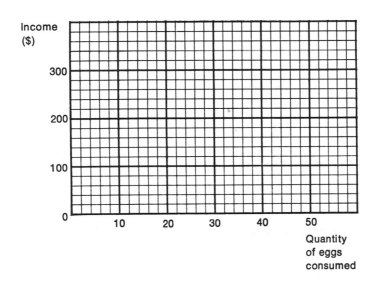

5. Describe the factors that will influence the shape of a consumer's Engel curve for a particular good.

6. Describe what is meant by a price-consumption curve. How can it be used to help determine the individual demand curve?

7. In the case of John Jones, the relationship between the price of eggs and the amount that he will purchase is shown below:

Price of eggs (cents per dozen)	Quantity of eggs consumed per week
50	15
60	14
70	13
80	12
90	11
100	10

Plot John Jones's individual demand curve for eggs in the graph below:

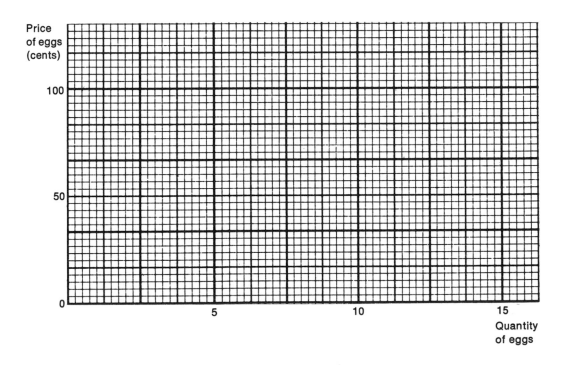

8. Suppose that a 1 percent increase in the price of pork chops results in Mrs. Smith's buying 3 percent fewer pork chops per week. What is the price elasticity of demand for pork chops on the part of Mrs. Smith? Is her demand for pork chops price-elastic or price-inelastic? Will an increase in the price of pork chops result in an increase, or a decrease, in the total amount of money that she spends on pork chops?

9. Explain what is meant by the "substitution effect" and the "income effect." Can the substitution effect be positive? Can the income effect be positive?

10. Explain the difference between normal and inferior goods. What is Giffen's paradox?

11. Explain the meaning of consumer's surplus. How was this concept used in RAND's analysis of New York's water problem?

12. *a*. Suppose Mrs. Smith's utility function can be described by $U = Q_c Q_p$, where U is her utility, Q_c is the amount of corn she consumes, and Q_p is the amount of potatoes she consumes. Draw her indifference curve when $U = 10$.

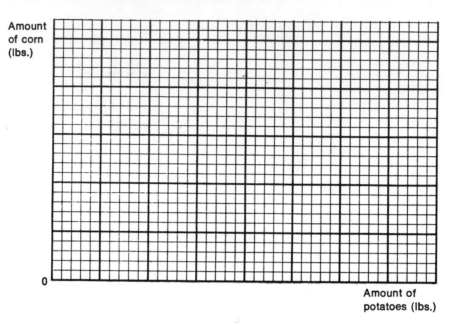

Amount of corn (lbs.)

0

Amount of potatoes (lbs.)

b. Suppose that the total amount of money she can spend on these two commodities is $100 and the price of corn is $1 per lb. How many potatoes will she buy if potatoes are 50 cents per lb.?

c. How much corn will she buy under these circumstances?

13. (*Advanced*) Derive a formula for Mrs. Smith's demand curve for potatoes. Let the price of potatoes be P_p and the price of corn be P_c. Let the total amount she spends on these two commodities be I. And assume that her utility function is $U = Q_c Q_p$.

14. What is the difference between a Laspeyres index and a Paasche index? How is each index useful?

15. The Federal government is interested in purchasing two types of antipollution equipment. After extensive tests, government officials are convinced that two units of type A equipment are as effective as one unit of type B equipment. Assuming that the officials want to reduce pollution, draw their indifference curves for the two types of equipment.

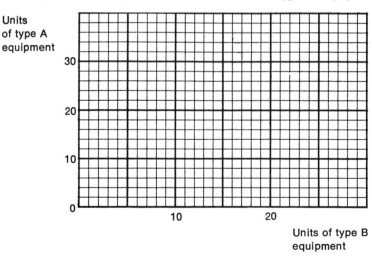

16. Assuming that the government has $20 million to spend on either type A equipment, type B equipment, or a combination of both, draw the relevant budget line, and indicate the optimal choice of type of equipment if a unit of type A equipment costs $1 million and a unit of type B equipment costs $2.5 million.

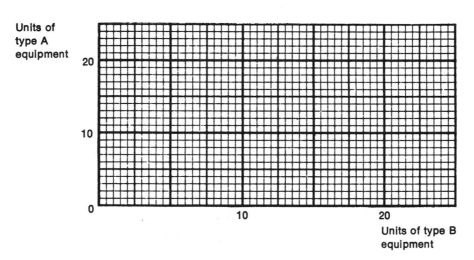

Completion Questions

1. The substitution effect is always _____.

2. Cost-of-living indexes have often been closely associated with _____.

3. An Engel curve is the relationship between the _____ and _____ _____.

4. The demand for a commodity is said to be price _____ if the elasticity of demand exceeds one.

5. The demand for a commodity is said to be price _____ if the elasticity of demand is less than one.

6. The demand for a commodity is said to be of _____ if the price elasticity of demand is equal to one.

7. The total effect of a change in price is obviously the sum of the _____ effect and the _____ effect.

8. If the consumer is in equilibrium and if the price of good X is $2 and the price of good Y is $1, then the marginal rate of substitution of good X for good Y must equal _____.

9. If increases in real income result in increases in the consumption of a good, this good is a _____ good.

-33-

10. If you can buy a good for $5 but you would be willing to pay as much as $50, the consumers' surplus is $_____.

True or False

_____ 1. The income-consumption curve is of no use in determining the Engel curve.

_____ 2. The price-consumption curve is of use in determining the individual demand curve.

_____ 3. A consumer's demand curve for a commodity generally will shift if his income changes.

_____ 4. A consumer's demand curve for a commodity generally will shift if the prices of other commodities change.

_____ 5. A consumer's demand curve for a commodity generally will shift if the consumer's tastes change a great deal.

_____ 6. The price elasticity of demand is measured by the slope of the demand curve.

_____ 7. If a good is price-elastic, a decrease in its price will result in a decrease in the amount of money spent on it.

_____ 8. If a good is price-elastic, an increase in its price will result in a decrease in the amount of money spent on it.

_____ 9. If the demand for a good is of unitary elasticity, the same amount of money is spent on it regardless of its price.

_____ 10. Giffen's paradox is a frequent occurrence.

_____ 11. Consumer's surplus can never be positive.

_____ 12. The Paasche index is always better than the Laspeyres index.

Multiple Choice

1. The substitution effect must always be
   a. positive.
   b. negative.
   c. zero.

2. The income effect
   a. must always be negative.
   b. must always be positive.
   c. can be positive or negative.

3. Normal goods experience an increase in consumption when
   a. real income increases.
   b. real income falls.
   c. price rises.
   d. price falls.

4. The Laspeyres index
   a. measures the change in the cost of the market basket purchased in the original year.
   b. measures the change in the cost of the market basket purchased in the later year.
   c. always exceeds 1.
   d. always is less than 1.

5. The Paasche index
   a. measures the change in the cost of the market basket purchased in the original year.
   b. measures the change in the cost of the market basket purchased in the later year.
   c. always exceeds 1.
   d. always is less than 1.

CHAPTER 4 Market Demand

Key Concepts

Market

Market demand curve

Price elasticity of demand

Point elasticity

Arc elasticity

Income elasticity of demand

Engel's law

Cross elasticity of demand

Substitute

Complement

Total revenue

Marginal revenue

Marginal revenue curve

Industry demand curve

Firm demand curve

Perfect competition

Identification problem

Direct experimentation

Consumer clinics

Horizontal demand curve

The Demand for Oranges: A Case for Discussion

In 1962, the Economic Research Service of the U.S. Department of Agriculture reported the results of a study of the effects of the price of various types of oranges on the rate at which they were purchased.* In particular, three types of oranges were studied: (1) Florida Indian River, (2) Florida Interior, and (3) California. In nine test stores in Grand Rapids, Michigan, the researchers varied the price of each of these types of oranges for a month. The effect of a 1 percent increase in the price of each type of orange on the rate of purchase of this and each of the other types of oranges is shown in Table 1. For example, a 1 percent increase in the price of Florida Indian River oranges (holding other prices constant) seemed to result in a 3.1 percent

Table 1: Results of Study

A 1 percent increase in the price of:	Results in the following percentage change in the rate of purchase of:		
	Florida Indian River	Florida Interior	California
Florida Indian River	−3.1	+1.6	+0.01
Florida Interior	+1.2	−3.0	+0.1
California	+0.2	+0.1	−2.8

*M. Godwin, W. Chapman, and W. Manley, *Competition Between Florida and California Valencia Oranges in the Fresh Market*, Department of Agriculture, December 1965. This paper is also summarized in G. Stokes, *Managerial Economies: A Casebook*, New York: Random House, 1969. I have changed the numbers slightly.

decrease in the rate of purchase of Florida Indian River oranges, a 1.6 percent increase in the rate of purchase of Florida Interior oranges, and a 0.01 increase in the rate of purchase of California oranges.

What seems to be the price elasticity of demand for each type of orange? What seems to be the cross elasticity of demand for each pair of types of oranges? Which types of oranges seem to be the closest substitutes? Of what use might these results be to orange producers? How accurate do you think that this study was? What improvements would you make in it?

Problems and Essays

1. According to Richard Tennant, "The consumption of cigarettes is . . . [relatively] insensitive to changes in price. . . . In contrast, the demand for individual brands is highly elastic in its response to price. . . . In 1918, for example, Lucky Strike was sold for a short time at a higher retail price than Camel or Chesterfield and rapidly lost half its business."[*] Explain why the demand for a particular brand is more elastic than the demand for all cigarettes. If Lucky Strike raised its price by 1 percent in 1918, was the price elasticity of demand for its product greater than 2?

[*]R. Tennant, "The Cigarette Industry," in W. Adams, *The Structure of American Industry*, New York: Macmillan, 1961, p. 371.

2. According to the president of Bethlehem Steel,* the demand for steel is price inelastic because steel generally constitutes a very small percentage of the total cost of the product that includes it as a raw material. If this is the case, will a price increase result in an increase or decrease in the amount of money spent on steel?

3. What is meant by a market? How can one derive the market demand curve from the demand curves of the individuals comprising the market?

*W. Adams, "The Steel Industry," in *ibid.*, p. 164.

4. **What is the difference between the point elasticity of demand and the arc elasticity of demand?**

5. **Suppose that the relationship between the price of steel and the quantity of steel demanded is as follows:**

Price ($)	Quantity
1	8
2	7
3	6
4	5
5	4

What is the arc elasticity of demand when price is between $1 and $2? Between $2 and $3? Between $4 and $5?

6. Suppose that the demand curve for aluminum is DD′, as shown below. Provide a measure of the price elasticity of demand at price OP.

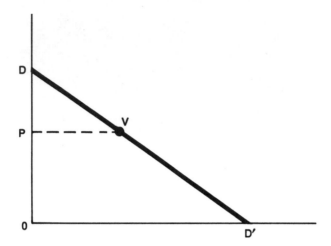

7. Discuss in detail the determinants of the price elasticity of demand.

8. Define the income elasticity of demand. How does the income elasticity of demand differ between luxuries and necessities? What does Engel's law state?

9. Define the cross elasticity of demand. How does the cross elasticity of demand differ between substitutes and complements?

10. If the relationship between price and quantity is as given below, derive the marginal revenue at various quantities and plot in the graph below the table.

Price	Quantity
$10	1
9	2
8	3
7	4
6	5
5	6
4	7
3	8
2	9

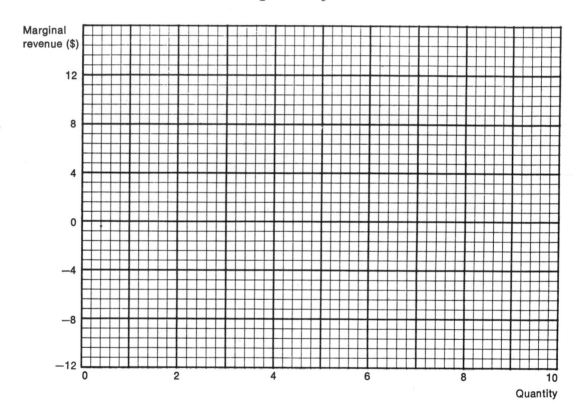

11. If the demand curve is DD′ in the graph below, draw in the marginal revenue curve.

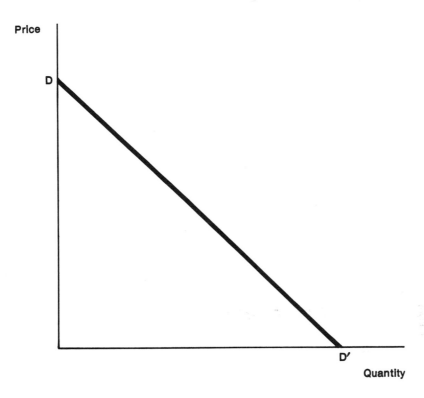

12. What does the firm's demand curve look like under perfect competition? Why?

13. Derive marginal revenue as a function of price (p) and the price elasticity of demand (n).

14. Discuss various ways that demand curves can be measured.

15. Suppose the Mayor of New York asked you to advise him concerning the proper fare that should be charged by the New York City subway. In what way might information concerning the price elasticity of demand be useful?

16. Suppose you are a business consultant and you become convinced that the U. S. steel industry underestimates the price elasticity of demand for steel. In what way might this information be useful to the steel companies? To the public?

17. Suppose you are a trustee of a major university. At a meeting of the board of trustees, one university official argues that the demand for places at this university is completely inelastic. As evidence, he cites the fact that, although the university has doubled its tuition in the last decade, there has been no appreciable decrease in the number of students enrolled. Do you agree? Comment on his argument.

18. Studies from cross-section data indicate that the income elasticity of demand for servants in the United States exceeds 1.00. Yet the number of servants has been decreasing during the last 50 years, while incomes have risen in the United States. How can these facts be reconciled?

19. *a.* According to Gregory Chow of I.B.M., the price elasticity of demand for automobiles in the United States is 1.2, and the income elasticity of demand for automobiles is 3.0. What would be the effect of a 3 percent decline in auto prices on the quantity of autos demanded, assuming Chow's estimates are right?

   b. What would be the effect of a 2 percent increase in income?

20. According to the Swedish economist Herman Wold's estimates, the income elasticity of demand for liquor is about 1.00. If you were an executive of a liquor firm, of what use might this fact be to you in forecasting sales?

21. According to Rex Daly of the Department of Agriculture, the price elasticity of coffee is about 0.25 to 0.30, and the income elasticity of demand is about 0.23. Suppose you were an economist for the coffee industry. How could you use this information to help forecast coffee sales in the United States?

22. According to Professor M. L. Burstein, the price elasticity of demand for refrigerators is between 1.00 and 2.00, and the income elasticity of demand is between 1.00 and 2.00. Compare these elasticities with those for coffee (in question 21). Why are the results for refrigerators so different from those for coffee?

23. *a.* According to S. Sackrin of the U. S. Department of Agriculture, the price elasticity of demand for cigarettes is between 0.3 and 0.4, and the income elasticity of demand is about 0.5. Suppose the Federal government, influenced by findings that link cigarettes and cancer, were to impose a tax on cigarettes that tripled their price. What effect would this have on cigarette consumption?

b. Suppose a brokerage house advised you to buy cigarette stocks because, if incomes rose by 50 percent in the next decade, cigarette sales would be bound to spurt enormously. What would be your reaction to this advice?

Completion Questions

1. If the cross elasticity of demand between goods X and Y is positive, these goods are classified as _____.

2. The income elasticity of demand is the percentage change in quantity demanded resulting from a _____ change in money income.

3. Luxury goods are generally assumed to have a _____ income elasticity of demand.

4. If a commodity has many close substitutes, its demand is likely to be _____ _____.

5. The price elasticity of demand equals _____.

6. Engel's law states that _____.

7. The demand curve for the individual firm under perfect competition is _____.

8. The price elasticity of demand is generally _____ in the long run than in the short run.

9. The total amount of money spent by consumers on a commodity equals the industry's ____ _____.

10. The _____ curve shows marginal revenue at various quantities of output.

11. If the industry is not perfectly competitive, the firm's demand curve will not be _____ _____.

12. Direct experimentation can be a _____ way to obtain data concerning a firm's or product's demand curve.

True or False

_____ 1. Summing horizontally the individual demand curves for all of the consumers in the market will produce the demand curve for the market.

_____ 2. The demand curve for an individual firm under perfect competition is downward sloping.

_____ 3. The market demand curve for a product under perfect competition is horizontal.

_____ 4. The demand for salt and pepper is likely to be price elastic.

_____ 5. In general, demand is likely to be more inelastic in the long run than in the short run.

_____ 6. The income elasticity of demand for food is very high.

_____ 7. It is always true that $n_{xy} = n_{yx}$.

_____ 8. The direct approach of simply asking people how much they would buy of a particular commodity is the best way to estimate the demand curve.

_____ 9. The identification problem is the problem of identifying the person who knows what the demand curve looks like.

_____ 10. The income elasticity of demand will always have the same sign regardless of the level of income at which it is measured.

_____ 11. Marginal revenue is the ratio of the value of sales to the amount sold.

_____ 12. When the demand curve is linear, the slope of the marginal revenue curve is twice (in absolute value) the slope of the demand curve.

Multiple Choice

1. Suppose that the demand curve is GG′ in the graph below:

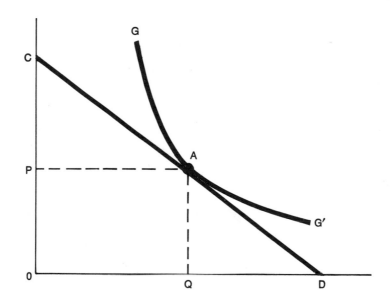

The price elasticity of demand is equal to
a. AD ÷ CA
b. AD ÷ AQ
c. CA ÷ PA
d. OP ÷ OQ

2. The demand for a good is price inelastic if
   a. the price elasticity is one.
   b. the price elasticity is less than one.
   c. the price elasticity is greater than one.

3. The relationship between marginal revenue and the price elasticity of demand is
   a. $MR = P \left(1 - \dfrac{1}{n}\right)$.
   b. $P = MR \left(1 - \dfrac{1}{n}\right)$.
   c. $P = MR(1 + n)$.
   d. $MR = P(1 + n)$.

4. A demand curve with unitary elasticity at all points is
   a. a straight line.
   b. a parabola.
   c. a hyperbola.

5. Suppose we are concerned with the relationships between the quantity of food demanded and aggregate income. It seems most likely that this relationship will look like:
   a. curve A below.
   b. curve B below.
   c. curve C below.

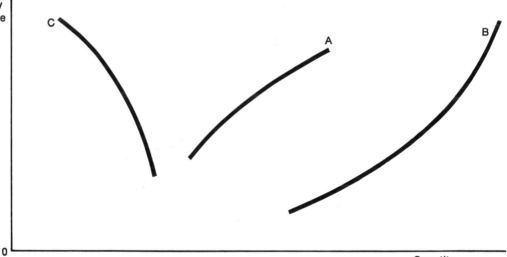

6. If goods X and Y are substitutes, the relationship between the quantity demanded of good X and the price of good Y should be like:

   a. curve A below.

   b. curve B below.

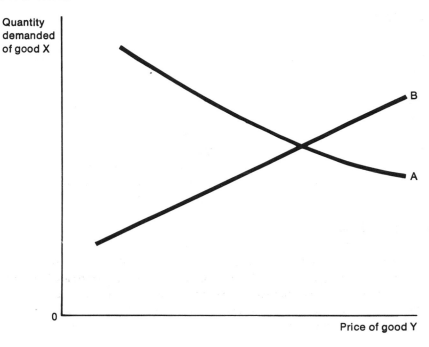

CHAPTER 5   The Firm and Its Technology

Key Concepts

Profit

Profit maximization

Technology

Input

Fixed input

Variable input

Short run

Long run

Production function

Marginal product

Average product

Law of diminishing marginal returns

Three stages of production

Isoquants

Economic region of production

Marginal rate of technical substitution

Increasing returns to scale

Decreasing returns to scale

Constant returns to scale

Cobb-Douglas production function

Problems and Essays

1. In the early 1880s, cigarette-rolling machinery became available. The new machines cut the cost of fabricating a cigarette in half. Assuming that capital and labor are the only inputs, what effect did this innovation have on the production function for cigarettes? Once the new machines were available, how did the optimal input combination differ from what it was before their introduction?

2. According to Joe Bain, there are important economies of scale in automobile production up to a plant size equaling about 5–10 percent of U.S. auto output. What are the implications of this fact for the number of auto companies that we are likely to find in the United States? In Chile? How would you go about obtaining data concerning economies of scale in some other industry?

3. If Q is the number of cars washed per hour and L is the number of men employed, a study of an auto laundry* found the following short-run relationship:

$$Q = -0.8 + 4.5L - .3L^2.$$

Does there appear to be diminishing marginal returns?

4. Discuss the limitations of profit maximization as an assumption concerning the motivation of the firm. What alternative assumptions can be made? Why does profit maximization remain the principal assumption made by economists?

*M. Spencer and L. Siegelman, *Managerial Economics*, Homewood, Ill.: Irwin, 1959, p. 204.

5. Discuss the nature of technology and the constraints it imposes on the firm's behavior. What are fixed inputs? Variable inputs?

6. Discuss the meaning of the production function. What is the short run? The long run? How does the production function in the short run differ from that in the long run?

7. *a.* Suppose the production function for a cigarette factory is as given below, there being only one input.

Amount of input (units per year)	Amount of output (units per year)
1	7
2	14.5
3	22
4	29
5	35
6	39
7	39

Plot the average product curve for the input in the graph below:

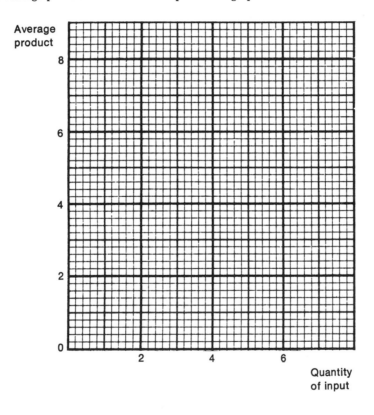

b. On the basis of the production function given in the first part of this question, plot the marginal product curve of the input.

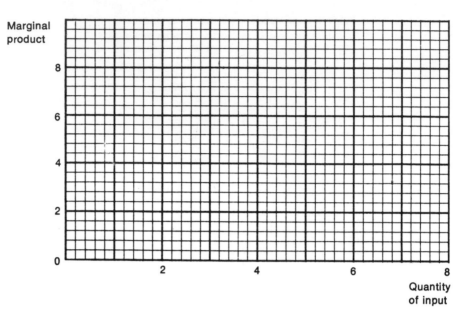

8. State the law of diminishing marginal returns. Indicate how this law is used to deduce the shape of the marginal product curve.

9. On the basis of the total product curve shown in the graph below, derive a measure of the average product and marginal product at OQ units of input by graphical techniques.

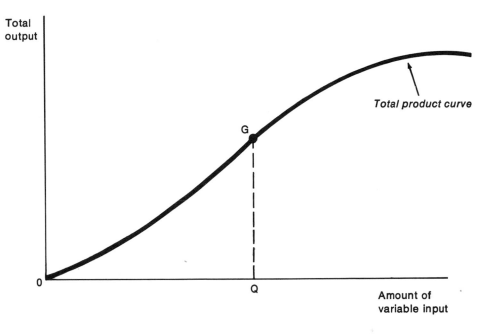

10. Describe the three stages of production. Show that the firm will not operate in stage III and that, if it can buy or sell all it wants at given input and output prices, it will try not to operate in stage I.

11. Describe an isoquant. Define the marginal rate of technical substitution.

12. Show that the marginal rate of technical substitution of labor for capital is equal to the ratio of the marginal product of labor to the marginal product of capital.

13. Describe what is meant by increasing returns to scale, decreasing returns to scale, and constant returns to scale. Discuss the factors that might be responsible for increasing returns to scale. Discuss the factors that might be responsible for decreasing returns to scale.

14. Describe the principal methods used to measure production functions in particular firms and industries. What are their limitations and advantages?

15. Discuss Herbert Simon's concept of decision-making in the firm. Also, discuss William Baumol's ideas on this subject.

16. Econometric studies of the cotton industry in India, indicate that the Cobb-Douglas production function can be applied, and that the exponent of labor is .92 and the exponent of capital is .12. Suppose that both capital and labor were increased by 1 percent. By what percent would output increase?

17. In the Cobb-Douglas production function, is the exponent of labor generally larger or smaller than that of capital?

18. Suppose that in a chemical plant, $Q = AL^\alpha K^\beta$, where Q is the output rate, L is the rate of labor input, and K is the rate of capital input. Statistical analysis indicates that $\alpha = .8$ and $\beta = .3$. The owner of the plant claims that there are increasing returns to scale in the plant. Is he right?

19. (*Advanced*) Suppose you are assured by the owner of an aluminum plant that his plant is subject to constant returns to scale, labor and capital being the only inputs. He claims that output per worker in his plant is a function of capital per worker only. Is he right?

Completion Questions

1. In the _____, all inputs are variable.

2. Herbert Simon is a proponent of _____ rather than maximization of profit.

3. The _____ production function can be written $Q = AI_1^{\alpha_1} I_2^{\alpha_2} I_3^{\alpha_3}$.

4. A fixed input is _____.

5. A variable input is _____.

6. In both the short run and the long run, a firm's productive processes generally permit substantial _____ in the proportions in which inputs are used.

7. The average product of an input is total product divided by _____
_____.

8. The marginal product of an input is the addition to total output due to _____
_____.

9. Underlying the law of diminishing marginal returns is the assumption that technology remains _____.

10. In stage I, the marginal product of the fixed input is _____.

11. In stage III, the marginal product of the variable input is _____.

12. Two isoquants can never _____.

True or False

_____ 1. An isoquant is analogous to the budget line in the theory of consumer demand.

_____ 2. The marginal rate of technical substitution equals minus one times the slope of the isoquant.

_____ 3. Isoquants are concave.

_____ 4. All production functions exhibit constant returns to scale.

_____ 5. Increasing returns to scale can occur because of the difficulty of coordinating a large enterprise.

_____ 6. Whether there are increasing, decreasing, or constant returns to scale in a particular case is an empirical question.

_____ 7. Statistical studies of production functions are hampered by the fact that available data do not always represent technically efficient combinations of inputs and outputs.

_____ 8. The only goal of any firm is to maximize profits.

_____ 9. Economists generally assume that firms maximize profits.

_____ 10. The concept of profit maximization is well defined in an uncertain world.

_____ 11. The production function is not closely related to a firm's or industry's technology.

_____ 12. The law of diminishing marginal returns applies to cases where there is a proportional increase in all inputs.

Multiple Choice

1. Suppose that the production function is as follows:

Quantity of output per year	Quantity of input per year
2	1
5	2
9	3
12	4
14	5
15	6
15	7
14	8

The average product of the input when 7 units of the input are used is
   a. 7.
   b. 15.
   c. 2 1/7.
   d. 7/15.

2. If the production function is as given in question 1, the marginal product of the input when between 1 and 2 units of the input is used is
   a. 2.
   b. 5.
   c. 3.
   d. 4.

3. If the production function is as given in question 1, the marginal product of the input begins to decline
   a. after 3 units of input are used.
   b. after 2 units of input are used.
   c. after 4 units of input are used.
   d. after 7 units of input are used.

4. If the production function is as given in question 1, the marginal product of the input is negative when more than
   a. 7 units of input are used.
   b. 6 units of input are used.
   c. 5 units of input are used.
   d. 4 units of input are used.

5. If the production function is as given in question 1, Stage III of the production process begins when more than
   a. 7 units of input are used.
   b. 6 units of input are used.
   c. 5 units of input are used.
   d. 4 units of input are used.

6. The marginal product equals the average product when the latter is
   a. 1/2 of its maximum value.
   b. 1/4 of its maximum value.
   c. equal to its maximum value.
   d. 1 1/2 times its maximum value.

7. A firm's aspiration level is
   a. its profits last year.
   b. the boundary between "satisfactory" and "unsatisfactory" outcomes.
   c. its highest previous profit level.
   d. related to the shoe size of the firm's president.

CHAPTER 6 Optimal Input Combinations and Cost Functions

Key Concepts

Isocost curve

Alternative cost

Opportunity cost

Social cost

Private cost

Explicit cost

Implicit cost

Cost function

Total fixed cost

Total variable cost

Total cost

Average fixed cost

Average variable cost

Average cost

Marginal cost

Break-even chart

Long-run average cost curve

Long-run marginal cost curve

Statistical cost functions

Problems and Essays

1. Based on results obtained by Harold Cohen,* the total cost of operating a hospital can be approximated by $4,700,000 + .00013 X^2, where X is the number of patient days (a crude measure of output). Derive an expression for the relationship between the cost per patient day and the number of patient days. How big must a hospital be (in terms of patient days) to minimize the cost per patient day?

*H. Cohen, "Hospital Cost Curves with Emphasis on Measuring Patient Care Output," in H. Klarman, *Empirical Studies in Health Economics*, Baltimore, Md.: Johns Hopkins, 1970.

2. J. A. Nordin[*] found the following relationship between an electric light and power plant's fuel costs (C) and its eight-hour output as a percent of capacity (Q):

$$C = 16.68 + 0.125\,Q + .00439Q^2.$$

When Q increases from 50 to 51, what is the increase in the cost of fuel for this electric plant? Of what use might this result be to the plant's managers?

3. Show that a firm will maximize output—for a given outlay—by distributing its expenditures among various inputs in such a way that the marginal product of a dollar's worth of any input is equal to the marginal product of a dollar's worth of any other input that is used.

[*] J. A. Nordin, *Econometrica*, July 1947.

4. Suppose that capital and labor are the only inputs used by a printing plant and that capital costs $1 a unit and labor costs $2 a unit. Draw the isocost curves corresponding to an outlay of $200 and $300.

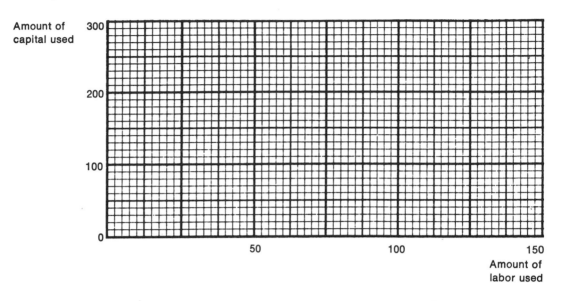

5. Discuss the reasons why the firm, if it is to minimize the cost of producing a given output, must equate the marginal rate of technical substitution and the input-price ratio.

6. Discuss the nature and importance of the opportunity cost, or alternative cost doctrine.

7. What are the differences between private and social costs? Illustrate your answer with cases of environmental pollution.

8. What are the differences between explicit and implicit costs? Why do economists bother with implicit costs?

9. What is the difference between the short run and the long run? What is the difference between fixed inputs and variable inputs?

10. *a.* Suppose that a steel firm's costs are as shown below:

Units of output	Total fixed cost	Total variable cost
0	$500	0
1	500	50
2	500	90
3	500	140
4	500	200
5	500	270
6	500	350
7	500	450
8	500	600

Draw the firm's total fixed cost function below:

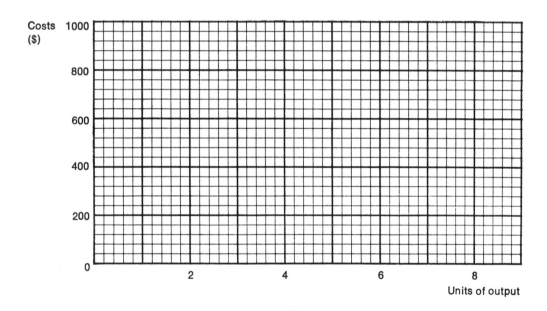

b. Draw the firm's total variable cost function below:

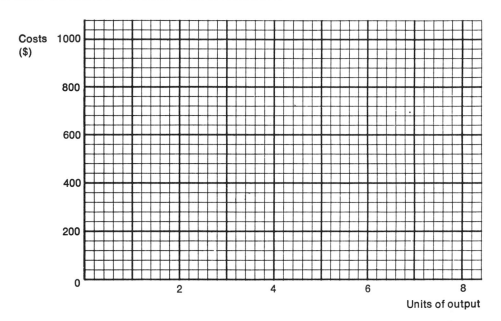

c. Draw the firm's total cost function below:

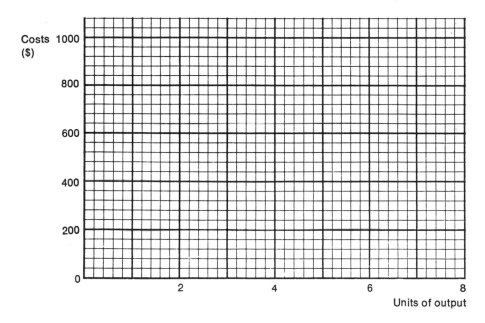

d. Draw the firm's average fixed cost function below:

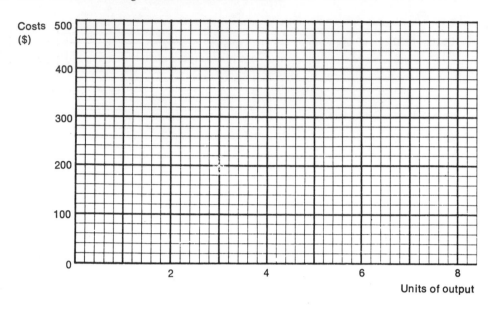

e. Draw the firm's average variable cost function below:

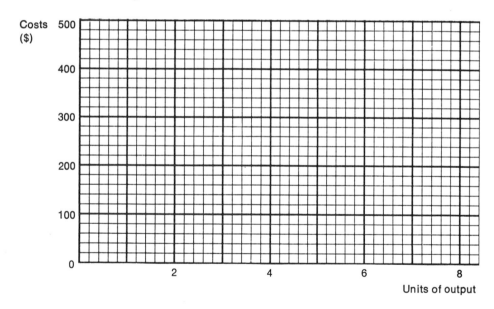

f. Draw the firm's average total cost function below:

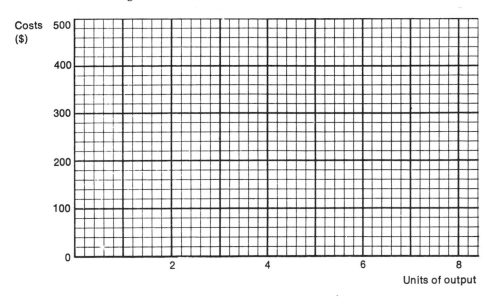

g. Draw the firm's marginal cost function below:

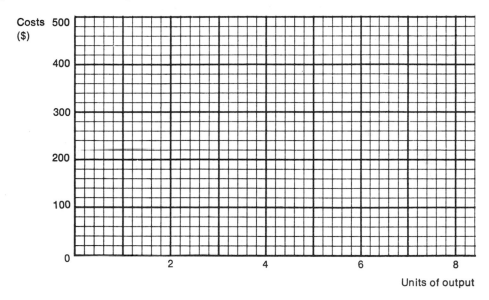

11. Suppose that you are a consultant to a firm that publishes books. Suppose that the firm is about to publish a book that will sell for $10 a copy. The fixed costs of publishing the books are $5000; the variable cost is $5 a copy. What is the break-even point for this book?

12. If the price were $8 rather than $10 in the previous problem, what would be the break-even point?

13. *a*. Suppose that a steel plant's production function is $Q = 5L\,K$, where Q is its output rate, L is the amount of labor it uses per period of time, and K is the amount of capital it uses per period of time. Suppose that the price of labor is $1 a unit and the price of capital is $2 a unit. The firm's vice president for manufacturing hires you to figure out what combination of inputs the plant should use to produce 20 units of output per period. What advice would you give him?

b. Suppose that the price of labor increases to $2 per unit. What effect will this have on output per unit of labor?

14. *a.* According to Joel Dean's classic study of a hosiery mill, total cost equaled $2936 + 1.998 Q, where Q is output. How does marginal cost behave, according to this finding?

b. How does average cost behave, according to this finding?

c. What factors could account for Dean's results?

15. According to Frederick Moore, engineers sometimes rely on the so-called ".6 rule" which states that the increase in cost is given by the increase in capacity raised to the .6 power. That is,

$$C_2 = C_1 \, (X_2/X_1)^{.6}$$

where C_1 and C_2 are the costs of two pieces of equipment and X_1 and X_2 are their respective capacities. Does the .6 rule imply economies of scale?

16. According to many econometric studies of long-run average cost in various industries, the long-run average cost curve tends to be L-shaped. For example, this is one of the conclusions reached by A. A. Walters in his well-known review article. Does this mean that there are constant returns to scale at all levels of output?

Completion Questions

1. If it minimizes cost, a firm will produce at a point where the isocost curve is _____ _____ to the isoquant.

2. Plant and equipment of a firm are _____ in the short run.

3. Total cost equals _____ plus variable cost.

4. Average cost must equal marginal cost at the point where average cost is a _____.

5. The long-run total cost equals output times _____.

6. _____ include opportunity costs of resources owned and used by the firm's owner.

7. An important criticism of cross-section studies of cost functions is that they sometimes are subject to the _____.

8. The determinants of the shape of the long-run average cost curve are _____ _____.

9. The total variable cost curve turns up beyond some output level because of the _____ _____.

10. The marginal cost curve turns up beyond some output level because of the _____ _____.

11. Average variable cost equals the price of the product divided by _____ _____, if the price of the product is constant.

12. Marginal cost equals the price of the product divided by _____ _____, if the price of the product is constant.

True or False

_____ 1. A firm cannot vary the quantity of labor inputs in the short run.

_____ 2. Costs that have already been incurred are important factors in making production decisions.

_____ 3. The opportunity cost doctrine says that the production of one good may reduce the cost of another good.

_____ 4. The marginal rate of technical substitution of labor for capital is the marginal product of capital divided by the marginal product of labor.

_____ 5. When the firm has constructed the scale of plant that is optimal for producing a given level of output, long-run marginal cost will equal short-run marginal cost at that output.

_____ 6. The shape of the long-run average cost function is due primarily to the law of diminishing marginal returns.

_____ 7. Average cost must exceed marginal cost at the point where average cost is a minimum.

_____ 8. The break-even point lies well above the output level that must be reached if the firm is to avoid losses.

_____ 9. Whether or not an industry is a natural monopoly depends on the long-run average cost curve and the industry demand curve.

_____ 10. Empirical studies often indicate the short-run average cost curve is S-shaped.

Multiple Choice

1. The curve in the graph below has the shape of
   a. marginal cost curve.
   b. average variable cost curve.
   c. average fixed cost curve.

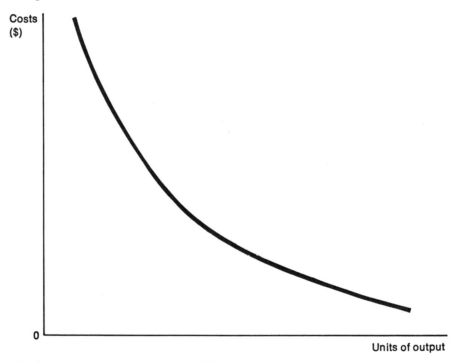

2. The firm's cost functions are determined by
   a. the price of its product.
   b. its assets.
   c. its production function.
   d. the age of the firm.

3. The following industry is a natural monopoly:
   a. cigarette industry.
   b. publishing industry.
   c. drug industry.
   d. electric power industry.

4. The curve shown below is
   a. an isoquant.
   b. an isocost curve.
   c. an average cost curve.
   d. a marginal cost curve.

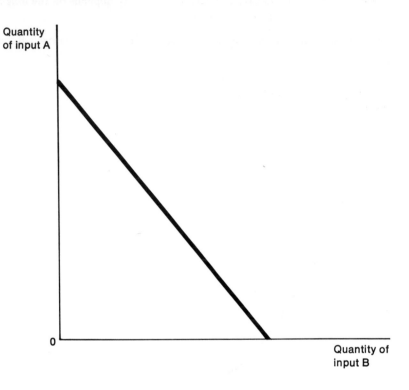

CHAPTER 7 Optimal Production Decisions and Linear Programming

Key Concepts

Product transformation curve
Marginal rate of product transformation
Isorevenue line
Linear programming
Process
Activity level

Constraints
Objective function
Isoprofit curves
Extreme points
Dual problem
Shadow prices
Simplex method

Problems and Essays

1. Suppose that you own a car wash and that its total cost function is:

$$C = 20 + 2Q + .3\,Q^2,$$

where C is total cost (in dollars) per hour and Q is number of cars washed per hour. Suppose that you receive $5 for each car that is washed. What is the optimal number of cars to wash per hour? What is the maximum profit that you can obtain?

2. Suppose once again that you are the owner of the car wash described in the previous problem. If the price you receive for each car wash falls from $5 to $2, will you continue to stay in operation? Why or why not?

3. In the car wash described in the preceding problems, how might you apply linear programming? What sorts of problems might it help you to solve?

4. *a.* Suppose that a perfectly competitive firm's total costs are as follows:

Output rate	Total cost
0	$10
1	12
2	15
3	19
4	24
5	30

If the price of the product is $5, how many units of output should the firm produce?

b. Draw the firm's total costs and total revenues in the graph below:

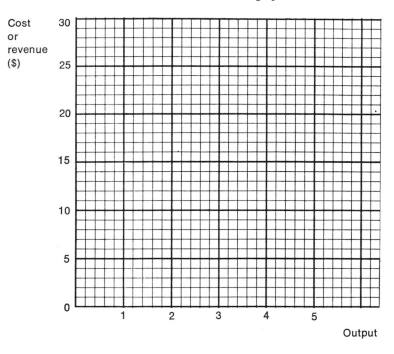

c. Draw the firm's marginal cost curve in the graph below, and find the output where price equals marginal cost.

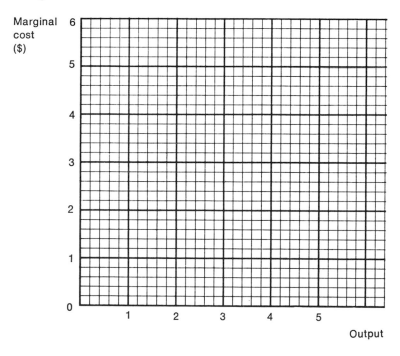

5.   Show why the firm will continue to produce so long as price exceeds average variable cost, even if it is smaller than average total cost.

6.   Discuss what is meant by the product transformation curve and how this curve can help to show how much of each product a firm should produce.

7. If the price of product 1 is $2 and the price of product 2 is $3, draw in the graph below the isorevenue line corresponding to a revenue of $200.

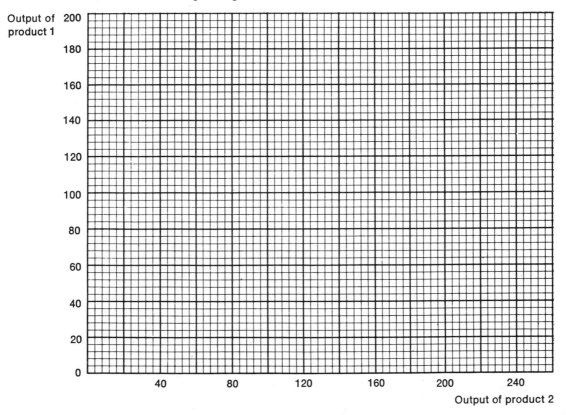

Output of product 2

8. Explain how the firm's production decision can be viewed as a linear programming problem. Describe the advantages of looking at it as a linear programming problem.

9.*a.* Suppose that there are two inputs, machine-hours of finishing capacity and man-hours of labor. If there are at most 2000 machine-hours and 200 man-hours available per week, draw the set of feasible input combinations in the graph below:

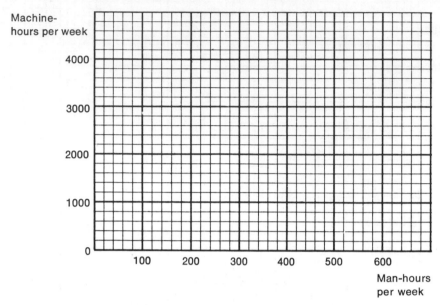

b. Suppose that one process utilizes 1 machine-hour and 1 man-hour to produce a unit of output. Graph the ray depicting this process below:

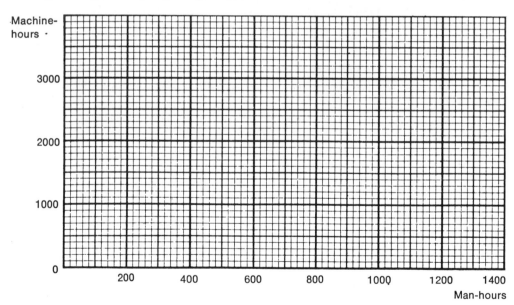

c. Suppose that another process utilizes 1/2 machine-hour and 2 man-hours to produce a unit of output, and that still another process utilizes 2 machine-hours and 1/2 man-hours to produce a unit of output. Graph the rays for these additional two processes below.

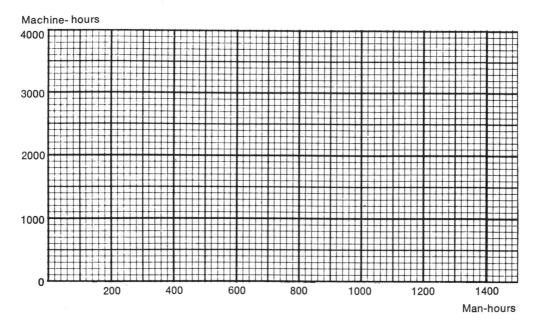

d. Graph the isoquant corresponding to 1000 units of output below (given the three processes described above).

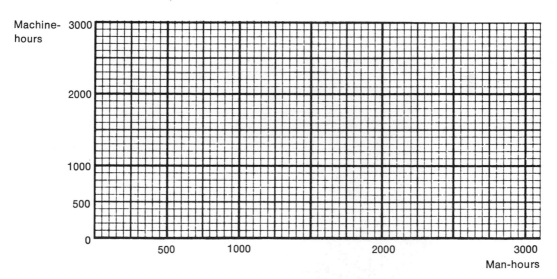

e. Suppose that the firm can rent all of the machine-hours it wants at $1 hour and all of the man-hours it wants at $1 an hour. Which process should it use to produce 1000 units of output?

10. Describe the meaning and usefulness of shadow prices.

11. Describe one of the ways in which linear programming has been used in the petroleum industry.

12. According to Robert Dorfman, "the essential simplification achieved in mathematical programming is the replacement of the notion of the production function by the notion of the process." Explain this in detail.

13. A family is composed of a husband and wife. The husband needs 3000 calories per day and the wife requires 2000 calories per day. The doctor says that these calories must be obtained by eating not less than a certain amount of fats and a certain amount of proteins. The family wants to minimize its food bill, but it does not want to violate the doctor's orders. Is this a linear programming problem? If so, what are the objective function and the constraints?

Completion Questions

1. Suppose that a cotton textile firm's total costs and total revenue are as follows:

Total output	Total cost	Total revenue
0	$30	0
1	33	$10
2	37	20
3	42	30
4	50	40
5	60	50
6	90	60

This firm's marginal cost between 2 and 3 units of output is _____ .

2. On the basis of the figures in question 1, this firm will produce _____ units of output.

3. This firm will make a loss of _____ .

4. If the firm shut down completely, it would make a loss of _____ .

5. The price of this firm's product is _____ .

6. At an output of between 4 and 5 units, the firm's marginal cost is _____ .

7. If price is less than marginal cost, decreases in output will _____ profit.

-92-

8. If price is more than marginal cost, increases in output will _____ profit.

9. The negative of the slope of the product transformation curve is _____
_____ .

10. In linear programming, each process uses inputs in _____ proportions.

True or False

_____ 1. Linear programming was invented in the nineteenth century.

_____ 2. Linear programming is a purely mathematical technique.

_____ 3. Linear programming seems to conform more closely than conventional analysis to the way that businessmen tend to view production.

_____ 4. Each process can be operated at only one activity level.

_____ 5. Linear programming works only when there are fewer than 10 constraints.

_____ 6. Isoquants are convex in the case of linear programming.

_____ 7. The optimal solution of a linear programming problem will occur at an extreme point.

_____ 8. The simplex method is a technique designed to determine how many processes the firm should utilize.

_____ 9. To every linear programming problem there corresponds a dual problem.

_____ 10. The solutions to the dual problem are the shadow prices.

Multiple Choice

1. The following graph shows the total cost and total revenue of a perfectly competitive firm.

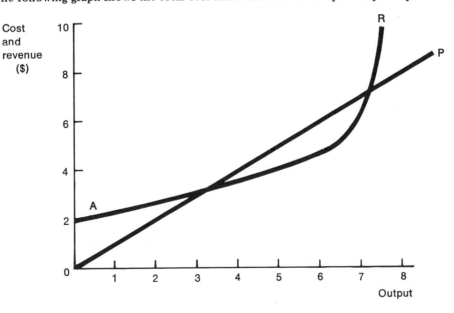

The line OP is
  a. the total cost curve.
  b. the total revenue curve.

2. The curve AR is
  a. the total cost curve.
  b. the total revenue curve.

3. The optimal output of the firm
  a. is less than 5.
  b. is more than 7.
  c. is 6 or 7.

4. In linear programming, isoquants are
  a. positively sloped.
  b. smooth.
  c. a series of connected line segments.

5. In linear programming, the objective function is
  a. A summary of the constraints.
  b. what you want to maximize or minimize.
  c. unimportant.

CHAPTER 8   Price and Output under Perfect Competition

Key Concepts

Market structure
Perfect competition
Market period
Supply curve in the short run
Equilibrium price
Equilibrium output
Economic profit
Entry of firms
Exit of firms
Long-run equilibrium of the firm

Constant cost industries
Increasing cost industries
Decreasing cost industries
External economies
Path to equilibrium
Cobweb theorem
Support price
Production quota
Brannan plan

Price Regulation: A Case for Discussion

Until 1954, the Federal Power Commission had no responsibility to regulate the price of natural gas. In that year, it was charged with this responsibility by the Supreme Court. In response to its new responsibility, the Commission established "area prices" for each of twenty-three natural gas producing regions of the United States. Any producer of gas was allowed to agree to a contract for a price less than or equal to the "area price" for his region. If he wanted a higher price, he had to prove its "necessity and convenience" to the Commission. According to many observers, the Commission set these "area prices" in such a way as to keep the price of natural gas below its equilibrium level.

Using the simple tools of microeconomic theory, it is easy to understand what seems to have occurred. According to MIT's Paul MacAvoy and others, the supply curve of additional reserves of natural gas is like SS' in Figure 1, the demand curve for additional reserves of natural gas being DD'. The Federal Power Commission set a ceiling price of OP_c, which is below the equilibrium price of OP_e.

Suppose that you were a member of the Federal Power Commission. Would you see anything wrong or harmful in this situation? If so, what is the problem, and what policies might you adopt to handle this problem? In fact, have there been pressures for changes in natural gas regulation in recent years?

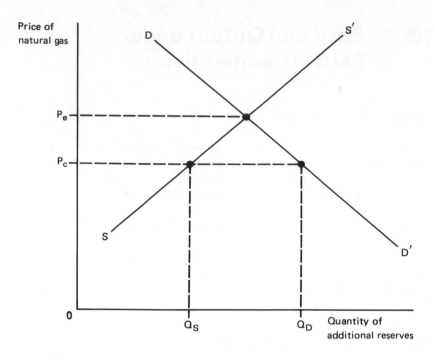

Problems and Essays

1. The Besser Manufacturing Company had only 465 employees in 1951 and sales of less than $15 million. Given that it is a small firm, can we be reasonably sure that it will have little or no control over the price of its product (concrete block machinery)?

2. In late 1962, Karl Fox* estimated that, based on a fairly typical farm situation in northeast Iowa, the most profitable number of dairy cows a farm operator should keep (at various expected prices of farm-separated cream) was as follows:

Expected price of cream (cents per pound)	Number of cows
60	2
80	4
100	6
120	11

If each cow yields the same amount of cream, what is the elasticity of supply of cream for this farm when the expected price of cream is about 90 cents per pound?

3. Describe the four basic conditions that define perfect competition. How often are they encountered in the real world?

*Farming, Farmers, and Markets for Farm Goods, Committee for Economic Development, 1962, p. 68.

4. Describe how equilibrium price is determined in a perfectly competitive market in the market period.

5. Suppose that the supply of a certain kind of paintings is fixed at 8 units, and that the demand curve for these paintings is as shown below. What is the equilibrium price for these paintings?

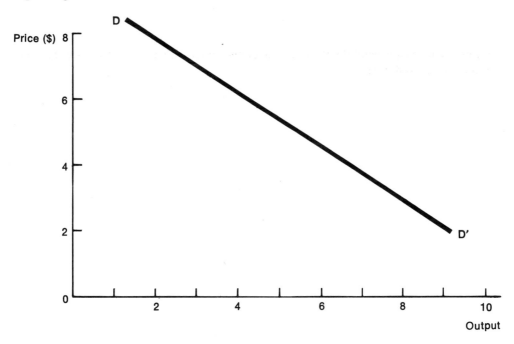

6. Show that the perfectly competitive firm's supply curve in the short run is its marginal cost curve.

7. If the supplies of inputs to the industry as a whole are perfectly elastic, show that the industry supply curve in the short run is the horizontal summation of the firm supply curves.

8. a. If the coal industry's demand and supply curves are as shown below, what are the equilibrium price and output?

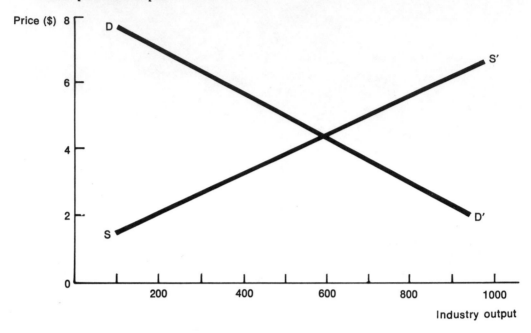

b. Why can't a price of $6 prevail in this market? Why can't a price of $2 prevail?

9. Describe the forces that determine whether there will be a net in-migration or out-migration of firms from a particular industry.

10. Describe the equilibrium conditions for the perfectly competitive firm in the long run.

11. Describe what is meant by constant cost industries.

12. Describe what is meant by increasing cost industries.

13. Describe what is meant by decreasing cost industries.

14. Given that price is currently at OP, show how price and output will move in succeeding periods, according to the cobweb theorem.

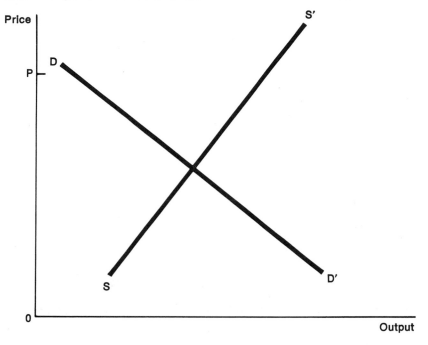

15. To what extent does the cotton textile industry conform to the assumptions of perfect competition?

16. Explain why, if we correct for changes in the price level resulting from over-all inflation, there was a declining trend in farm prices up to 1973.

17. Explain why farm prices vary between good times and bad to a much greater extent than nonfarm prices.

18. According to the U. S. Census Bureau, the largest four producers of rubber products accounted for about 50 percent of the industry's value added. Do you think that the perfectly competitive model will work as well in rubber products as in cotton textiles? Why or why not?

19. According to Marc Nerlove and W. Addison, the long-run elasticity of the supply of green peas is about 4.40. Of what use might this fact be to the Department of Agriculture?

20. According to Arthur Harlow of the Bonneville Power Administration, there is an important cycle in hog production. "Price preceded pig crop by one year, and slaughter followed the pig crop by a year. Prices were high when slaughter was low and vice versa." Is this sort of behavior consistent with the cobweb theorem?

21. According to D. Suits and S. Koizumi, the supply function for onions in the United States is $\log q = 0.134 + .0123\,t + 0.324 \log P - 0.512 \log C$, where q is the quantity supplied in a particular year, t is the year (less 1924), P is the price last season, and C is the cost index last season. Suppose that price is estimated by one forecaster to be 10 cents this season, whereas another says that it will be 11 cents. How much difference will this make in the quantity supplied next season?

Completion Questions

1. In the market period, quantity is set by _____ alone.

2. In the market period, price is set by _____ alone, given a fixed quantity.

3. In the long run, a perfectly competitive firm's equilibrium position is at the place where its long-run average cost equals _____ .

4. A decreasing cost industry has a _____ long-run supply curve.

5. An increasing cost industry has an _____ long-run supply curve.

6. A constant cost industry has a _____ long-run supply curve.

7. The supply curve in the market period is _____ .

8. At the optimal level of production, profit maximization requires that long-run marginal cost equals short-run _____ equals price.

9. If the supply curve is steeper than the demand curve, price tends to _____ , if the cobweb theorem holds.

10. According to the results of Nerlove and Addison, short-run supply elasticities tend to be _____ than long-run supply elasticities in American agriculture.

11. External economies may result in _____ that occur when the industry expands.

12. Increasing cost and constant cost industries are more _____ than decreasing cost industries.

True or False

_____ 1. In the short run, equilibrium price under perfect competition may be above or below average total cost.

_____ 2. In the long run, equilibrium price under perfect competition may be above or below average total cost.

_____ 3. The supply curve is a horizontal line in the market period.

_____ 4. The demand for a good is fixed in the market period.

_____ 5. Under perfect competition, one producer can produce a somewhat different good from other producers in his industry.

_____ 6. Under perfect competition, each firm must be careful not to produce too much and spoil the market.

_____ 7. One can derive the firm's supply curve in the short run by simply tracing out its average cost curve.

_____ 8. One can always derive the industry's supply curve by summing up the firm's marginal cost curves.

_____ 9. At the equilibrium price, price will equal marginal cost (for all firms that choose to produce) under perfect competition.

_____ 10. Under perfect competition, marginal cost is the same for all producers of a particular product in equilibrium.

_____ 11. Firms that appear to have lower costs than others often have superior resources or managements.

_____ 12. The Brannan plan may cost the Treasury more than the previous price supports and production controls.

Multiple Choice

1. The long-run average cost curve of a perfectly competitive firm is given below. Given that this curve does not shift, the long-run equilibrium output of the firm will be
   a. 4 units.
   b. 5 units.
   c. 6 units.
   d. 7 units.

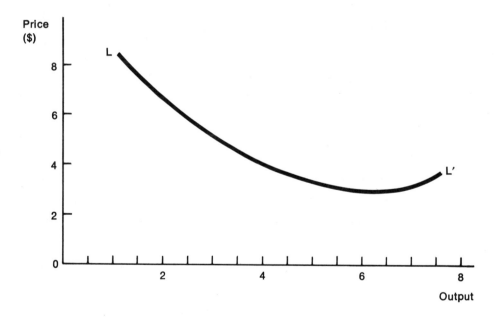

2. According to the cobweb theorem, the amount supplied of a commodity depends on
   a. this period's price.
   b. price in the previous period.
   c. expectations of future price.
   d. expectations of future demand.

3. If the demand curve shifts to the right (and if the supply curve is upward sloping), equilibrium price will
   a. decrease.
   b. increase.
   c. stay the same.

4. Recognizing that the assumptions of perfect competition never hold at all precisely, the perfectly competitive model is
   a. interesting but useless.
   b. not very interesting and not very useful.
   c. of considerable use nevertheless.

5. Under perfect competition, rivalry is
   a. impersonal.
   b. very personal and direct, advertising being important.
   c. nonexistent since the firms cooperate and collude.

CHAPTER 9 Price and Output under Pure Monopoly

Key Concepts

Monopoly
Natural monopoly
Patents
Market franchise
Multiplant monopoly
Bilateral monopoly
Price discrimination

First-degree price discrimination
Second-degree price discrimination
Third-degree price discrimination
Fair rate of return
Regulatory commissions
Value of plant

Subway Fares: A Case for Discussion

In the early 1950s, it was felt by many responsible citizens that the burden on the city budget due to the subway deficit was perhaps the single most important factor in New York City's financial problem. The increased operating cost resulting from the adoption of the forty-hour week, together with higher prices of materials, were expected to cause an operating deficit for 1951–52 of almost $30 million for the city's transit system.

In response to this problem, the question was raised of whether or not subway fares should be increased. William Vickrey of Columbia University was asked by the Mayor's Committee on Management Survey of the City of New York to make a study of this question. Vickrey made four estimates of the demand curve, each based on a different assumption regarding its form. In Case A, he assumed that equal absolute changes in fare result in equal absolute changes in traffic. In Case B, he assumed that equal absolute changes in fare result in equal percentage changes in traffic. In Case C, he assumed that equal percentage changes in fare result in equal absolute changes in traffic. And in Case D, he assumed that equal percentage changes in fare result in equal percentage changes in traffic.* His results are shown in Table 1.

Suppose that you were a member of the Mayor's Committee on Management Survey, and that you were presented the data in Table 1. How would these data be useful in deciding whether or not to raise the subway fare from the then-prevailing level of 10 cents? What additional data would you need in order to come to a conclusion of this score?

---

*This very brief sketch cannot do justice to Vickrey's study, which was concerned with many other important aspects of the problem. See W. Vickrey, *The Revision of the Rapid Transit Fare Structure of the City of New York*, Technical Monograph No. 3, Finance Project, Mayor's Committee on Management Survey of the City of New York, 1952.

Table 1. Alternative Estimates of Demand Schedule for Subway Travel, New York, 1952.

Fare (cents)	Case A Passengers	Case A Total revenue	Case B Passengers	Case B Total revenue	Case C Passengers	Case C Total revenue	Case D Passengers	Case D Total revenue
			(passengers and revenues in millions per year)					
5	1945	$ 97.2	1945	$ 97.2	1945	$ 97.2	1945	$ 97.2
10	1683	168.3	1683	168.3	1683	168.3	1683	168.3
15	1421	213.2	1458	218.7	1530	229.5	1547	232.0
20	1159	231.8	1262	252.4	1421	284.2	1457	291.5
25	897	224.2	1092	273.0	1347	336.8	1390	348.2
30	635	190.5	945	283.5	1278	383.4	1340	402.0

Source: W. S. Vickrey.

Problems and Essays

1. According to Milton Spencer,* the makers of methyl methacrylate used to sell it at 85 cents per pound for commercial purposes. However, for denture purposes, it was sold to the dental profession for $45 per pound. Assuming that there was no difference in quality, why would the producers of methyl methacrylate, DuPont and Rohm and Haas, find it profitable to charge different prices? In which of these markets (the commercial market or the dental market) do you think that the price elasticity of demand was lower?

*Managerial Economics, Homewood, Ill.: Irwin, 1968, p. 325.

2. According to Meyer, Peck, Stenason, and Zwick, trucks "have a comparative long-run marginal cost advantage over rails only on hauls of less than roughly 100 miles. Yet 97 percent of all manufactured goods ton-miles transported by common motor carriers in the early 1950's were on hauls of more than 100 miles."* What are the implications for resource allocation in transportation? What policies of the ICC help to account for this fact?

3. **Define pure monopoly. Is a monopolist subject to any kind of competition?**

*F. M. Scherer, *Industrial Market Structure and Economic Performance* Skokie, Ill.: Rand McNally, 1970, pp. 539-40.

4. What are some of the most important factors that give rise to monopoly?

5. How does the monopolist's demand curve differ from that of a perfectly competitive firm? How do his costs differ from those of a competitive firm?

6. *a.* Suppose that a monopolist's demand curve and total cost curve are as follows:

Output	Price ($)	Total cost ($)
1	10	20
2	9	21
3	8	22
4	7	23
5	6	24
6	5	26
7	4	29
8	3	32

Plot the monopolist's total revenue and total cost curves in the graph below:

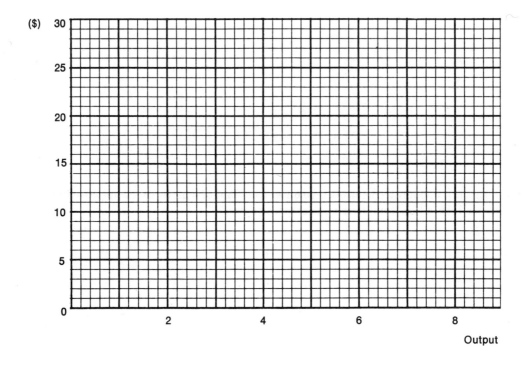

b. Plot the monopolist's marginal revenue and marginal cost curves in the graph below:

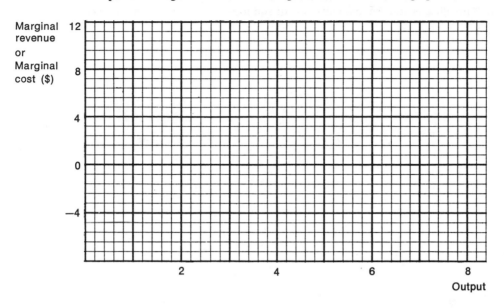

c. What output will maximize the monopolist's profit? Is this output the one where marginal cost equals marginal revenue? What price should the monopolist charge?

7. Show why a monopolist will always set his output at the point where marginal revenue equals marginal cost, if he maximizes profit and if price exceeds average variable cost.

8. Suppose that a monopolist has more than one plant. If he minimizes costs, how will he allocate production among the plants? Why?

9. Compare the long-run equilibrium of monopoly with that of perfect competition. How does output compare? How do costs compare? How does price compare?

10. Describe how, according to some economists, the welfare loss to society due to monopoly can be measured by the so-called "welfare triangle."

11. Are price and output determined exactly by the theory of bilateral monopoly? Where might this theory be of some relevance?

12. What is price discrimination? Under what circumstances is it feasible for a firm to practice discrimination? Under what circumstances is it profitable for the firm to practice price discrimination?

13. Under price discrimination, how does a monopolist decide how much to produce? How does he decide how to allocate this output among markets?

14. According to C. Emery Troxel, a general rate case is the common sort of regulatory "contest" in the Michigan telephone industry. What sorts of concepts and methods are used by these commissions in such cases?

15. *a.* Suppose that you are the owner of a metals producing firm that is an unregulated monopoly. After considerable experimentation and research you find that your marginal cost curve can be approximated by a straight line, $MC = 60 + 2Q$, where MC is marginal cost (in $) and Q is your output. Moreover, suppose that the demand curve for your product is $P = 100 - Q$, where P is the product price and Q is your output. If you want to maximize profit, what output should you choose?

b. What price should you charge?

16. a. Suppose that you are hired as a consultant to a firm producing ball bearings. This firm is a monopolist which sells in two distinct markets, one of which is completely sealed off from the other. The demand curve for the firm's output in the one market is $P_1 = 160 - 8Q$, where P_1 is the price of the product and Q_1 is the amount sold in the first market. The demand curve for the firm's output in the second market is $P_2 = 80 - 2Q_2$, where P_2 is the price of the product and Q_2 is the amount sold in the second market. The firm's marginal cost curve is $5 + Q$, where Q is the firm's entire output (destined for either market). The firm asks you to suggest what its pricing policy should be. How many units of output should it sell in the second market?

b. How many units of output should it sell in the first market?

17. Many industries—for example, the steel industry—claim that the demand for their product is price-inelastic. Suppose that you were able to bring together all of the firms in an industry and form a monopoly. Would you operate at a point on the demand curve where demand is price-inelastic?

18. According to Milton Friedman of the University of Chicago, it is preferable in cases of natural monopoly for society to tolerate private unregulated monopoly than to attempt to regulate natural monopolies. Do you agree?

19. The Aluminum Company of America (Alcoa) was the sole manufacturer of virgin aluminum ingot in the United States from its inception in the late nineteenth century until World War II. Suppose that in the 1920's you had had the power to break up Alcoa into several smaller firms. Would you have done so? Why?

20. According to Sir John Hicks, "the best of all monopoly profits is a quiet life." If so, how would this affect the theory of pure monopoly?

21. According to Henry C. Simons, "the great enemy of democracy is monopoly in all of its forms." Do you agree? Why or why not?

Completion Questions

1. The threat of potential competition often acts as a _____ on the policies of a monopolist.

2. A monopolist's demand curve is the same as the industry _____ .

3. For a monopolist, marginal revenue is _____ than price.

4. Under monopoly, there is not always a _____ relationship between price and output.

5. In the long run, a monopolistic firm will _____ incur losses, but it may make _____ .

6. Under multiplant monopoly, the monopolist will equalize the _____ of the output of each plant if he minimizes cost.

7. If the demand for the product shifts to the right, the monopolist _____ _____ increase price.

8. Price will be _____ under monopoly than under perfect competition.

9. Output will be _____ under monopoly than under perfect competition.

10. Average cost will be _____ under monopoly than under perfect competition.

11. Bilateral monopoly occurs when a monopolistic seller is confronted with _____

_____ .

12. Under bilateral monopoly, price and output are _____.

True or False

_____ 1. Price discrimination cannot occur unless consumers can be segregated into classes and the commodity cannot be transferred from one class to another.

_____ 2. Price discrimination always occurs when differences in price exist among roughly similar products, even when their costs are not the same.

_____ 3. Price discrimination is profitable even when the price elasticity of demand is the same among each class of consumer in the total market.

_____ 4. If a monopolist practices price discrimination, he does not set marginal revenue equal to marginal cost.

_____ 5. First-degree price discrimination occurs frequently, particularly in the auto industry.

_____ 6. Sometimes a commodity cannot be produced without price discrimination, for the industry would have to produce at a loss otherwise.

_____ 7. Commissions often try to set the price at the level at which it includes average total cost, including a "fair" rate of return on the firm's investment.

_____ 8. It is a simple matter to tell what is a "fair" rate of return and what is the value of a firm's investment.

_____ 9. The prewar aluminum industry was regarded by many observers as being a monopoly.

_____ 10. The telephone industry is subject to public regulation.

Multiple Choice

1. Monopolies can arise as a consequence of
   a. patents.
   b. control over the supply of a basic input.
   c. franchises.
   d. the shape of the long-run average cost curve.
   e. all of the above.

2. A monopolistic firm will expand its output when
   a. marginal revenue exceeds marginal cost.
   b. marginal cost exceeds marginal revenue.
   c. marginal cost equals marginal revenue.
   d. marginal revenue is negative.

3. A monopolist will never produce at a point where
   a. demand is price-inelastic.
   b. demand is price-elastic.

    c. marginal cost is positive.

    d. marginal cost is increasing.

4. A profit-maximizing monopolist, if he owns a number of plants, will always:

    a. produce some of his output at each plant.

    b. transfer output from plants with high marginal cost to those with low marginal cost.

    c. transfer output from plants with low marginal cost to those with high marginal cost.

    d. produce all of his output at a single plant and shut down the rest.

5. Suppose that the monopolist's marginal cost is constant in the relevant range and that his demand curve is downward-sloping and linear. Suppose that an excise tax is imposed on the monopolist's product. If he maximizes profit, he will increase his price by

    a. an amount less than the tax.

    b. an amount equal to the tax.

    c. an amount more than the tax.

    d. no amount at all.

6. To determine how a discriminating monopolist will allocate output between two classes of consumers, one must

    a. compare the marginal revenues in the classes.

    b. compare the prices in the classes.

    c. compare the slopes of the demand curves in the classes.

    d. compare the heights of the demand curves in the classes.

CHAPTER 10 Price and Output under Monopolistic Competition

Key Concepts

Monopolistic competition
Product differentiation
Product group
dd' demand curve
DD' demand curve
Representative firm

Product variation
Selling expenses
Ideal output
Ideal plant
Excess capacity

Problems and Essays

1. According to Mann, Henning, and Meehan,* there is a fairly substantial positive correlation between the ratio of advertising expenditure to sales in an industry and the percent of the industry's sales accounted for by the four largest firms. What factors may account for such a correlation?

*Journal of Industrial Economics, 1967.

2. According to one estimate,* perhaps a fourth of the 1963 sales of drug stores, liquor stores, and gasoline stations were made by firms whose costs were 10 percent higher than the optimum, the resulting annual cost being $775 million, or .13 percent of GNP. Why do such inefficiencies come about and persist?

3. What sorts of dissatisfaction with the theory of perfect competition and monopoly led to the theory of monopolistic competition? Who were the principal founders of the theory of monopolistic competition? When did their theories first appear?

* F. M. Scherer, *Industrial Market Structure and Economic Performance*, Skokie Ill.: Rand McNally, 1970, pp. 406–7.

4. Describe the basic assumptions underlying Chamberlin's theory of monopolistic competition.

5. Describe the two basic types of demand curves that play a fundamental role in the theory of monopolistic competition.

6. Describe the equilibrium conditions for price and output under monopolistic competition in the short run.

7. Describe the equilibrium conditions for price and output under monopolistic competition in the long run.

8. Describe how, according to Chamberlin's theory, firms determine the characteristics of their products. Describe too how they decide how much to spend on selling expenses.

9. What is meant by ideal output and ideal plant? Describe the reasoning leading to the conclusion that there will tend to be excess capacity under monopolistic competition.

10. Compare the long-run equilibrium of a monopolistically competitive industry with the long-run equilibria of perfectly competitive and monopolistic industries.

11. Discuss the criticisms of Chamberlin's theory of monopolistic competition by Stigler, Harrod, and others. How important do you think these criticisms are?

12. Give five real-world examples of industries in which there is product differentiation.

13. According to some economists, there are too many gas stations and grocery stores. Is this in keeping with the theory of monopolistic competition?

Completion Questions

1. Chamberlin's theory assumes that there are a _____ of firms and a _____ product.

2. The dd' demand curve assumes that other firms _____ their prices.

3. The DD' demand curve assumes that other firms make _____ changes in their price as the representative firm does.

4. Under monopolistic competition, the theory claims that _____ will be produced at a _____ price than under pure monopoly.

5. Under monopolistic competition, the theory suggests that _____ will be produced at a _____ price than under perfect competition.

6. It is difficult to compare perfect competition with monopolistic competition because the product is _____ under perfect competition but _____ under monopolistic competition.

7. In monopolistic competition, each firm expects its actions to have _____ on its competitors.

8. In short-run equilibrium in monopolistic competition, the dd' demand curve intersects the _____ at the output where marginal revenue equals marginal cost.

9. In long-run equilibrium in monopolistic competition, the long-run average cost curve is tangent to the _____ .

10. Excess capacity under monopolistic competition may be fairly small if the demand curve facing the monopolistically competitive firm is _____ .

True or False

_____ 1. Excess capacity is desirable and indicative of productive efficiency.

_____ 2. Monopolistic competition is likely to result in more firms and more brands than perfect competition.

_____ 3. Under monopolistic competition, firms can vary the characteristics of their products.

_____ 4. Chamberlin assumes that firms in the same product group under monopolistic competition have the same cost and demand curves.

_____ 5. The dd' demand curve is less elastic than the DD' demand curve.

_____ 6. Long-run equilibrium under monopolistic competition will be achieved when economic profits are zero.

_____ 7. Entry and exit under monopolistic competition are as free as they are under perfect competition.

_____ 8. Entry and exit have an influence on the DD' demand curve.

_____ 9. According to George Stigler, Chamberlin's definition of the group of firms in the product group is very ambiguous.

_____ 10. It is obvious that product differentiation is a waste and that all industries should standardize their products.

Multiple Choice

1. In the graph below, one of the curves is the dd′ demand curve and one is the DD′ demand curve. The dd′ demand curve is:
   a. AA′
   b. BB′

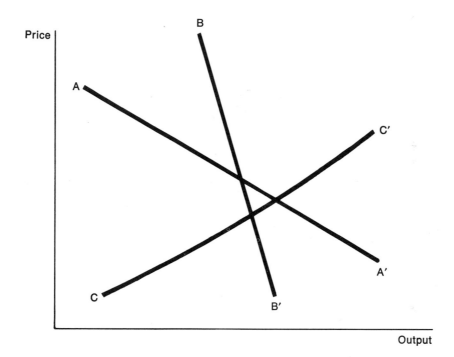

2. In the previous question, the DD′ demand curve is
   a. AA′
   b. BB′

3. Under monopolistic competition, a firm can use selling expenses to increase its profits. We know that such expenses are
   a. a social waste.
   b. entirely socially productive.
   c. large in many industries, but we are able to say little with confidence about their social productivity.

4. Given that a firm is in short-run equilibrium and UU' is the dd' demand curve, the equilibrium price is
   a. OP_0
   b. OP_1
   c. OP_2

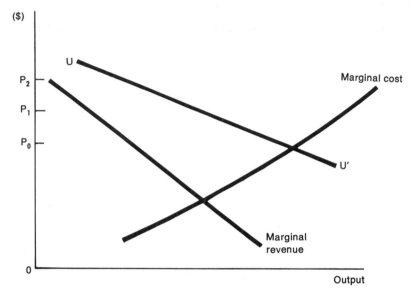

5. Suppose that a firm is in short-run equilibrium and WW' is the DD' demand curve, but the marginal revenue curve shown below is the marginal revenue curve based on the dd' demand curve. The equilibrium price would now be
   a. OP_3
   b. OP_4
   c. OP_5

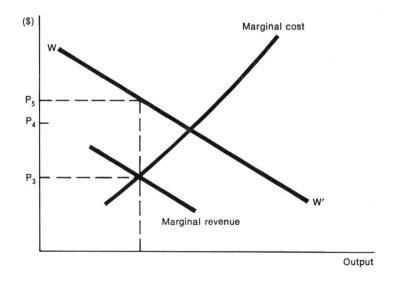

CHAPTER 11 Price and Output under Oligopoly

Key Concepts

Oligopoly
Pure oligopoly
Differentiated oligopoly
Collusion
Duopoly
Cournot model
Edgeworth model
Chamberlin Model
Kinked oligopoly demand curve
Nonprice competition
Theory of games

Player
Strategy
Payoff matrix
Minimax strategy
Mixed strategy
Cartel
Price leadership
Dominant firm
Barometric firm
Cost-plus pricing
Limit pricing

Problems and Essays

1. In its 1932 annual report,* Aluminium, Ltd. of Canada noted that "World stocks of aluminum are not excessively large. They are in firm hands and do not weigh unduly upon the world market." What did it mean by "firm hands?" Do you think that this phenomenon was at all related to the firmness of world aluminum prices during this period? Under perfect competition, do you think that aluminum prices would have remained fairly constant in the face of sharp reductions in sales during the Great Depression?

*F. M. Scherer, *Industrial Market Structure and Economic Performance*, Skokie, Ill.: Rand McNally, 1970, p. 156.

2. According to F. M. Scherer,* Reynolds and American share price leadership in cigarettes, U.S. Steel has often been the price leader in steel, Alcoa has led most frequently in virgin aluminum, American Viscose in rayon, DuPont in nylon and polyester fibers. What characteristics tend to distinguish price leaders from other firms? If you had to predict which of a number of firms in an industry was the price leader, what variables would you use to make the forecast?

3. What is meant by oligopoly? How does oligopoly arise? What is the difference between pure oligopoly and differentiated oligopoly?

*Ibid., p. 167.

4. Describe the Cournot model. Comment on the reasonableness of its assumptions.

5. Describe the Edgeworth model. Comment on the reasonableness of its assumptions.

6. Describe the Chamberlin model. In what respect is this model more reasonable than Cournot's or Edgeworth's?

7. What is meant by the kinked oligopoly demand curve? Does this theory explain the level of price? What does it help to explain?

8. Describe the elements of game theory. To what extent are two-person zero-sum games representative of actual market conditions?

9. Suppose the pay-off matrix is as given below. What strategy will firm I choose? What strategy will firm II choose?

Possible strategies for firm I	Possible strategies for firm II		
	1	2	3
	[Profits for firm I, or losses for firm II]		
A	$10	$9	$11
B	8	8.5	10

10. What are some of the criticisms of game theory? How important do these criticisms seem to be?

11. What is a cartel? How will a perfect cartel determine its price and output? Is it likely that a cartel will allocate output among its members so as to minimize total cost?

12. Why are cartels and collusive agreements inherently unstable? Document your answer with evidence from the electrical equipment conspiracy in the United States in the 1950s.

13. Describe the dominant-firm model of price leadership. How does it differ from the baro-metric-firm model?

14. What is meant by cost-plus pricing? Is the cost-plus model a complete model?

15. What are some important barriers to entry?

16. Describe the effects of an oligopolistic market structure on price, output, and profits.

17. *a*. Suppose that you are on the board of directors of an oil firm which is the dominant firm in the industry. That is, it lets all of the other firms, which are much smaller, sell all they want at the existing price. In other words, the smaller firms act as perfect competitors. Your firm, on the other hand, sets the price, which the other firms accept. The demand curve for your industry's product is $P = 300 - Q$, where P is the price of oil and Q is the total quantity demanded. The total amount supplied by the other firms is equal to Q_r, where $Q_r = 49 P$. If your firm's marginal cost curve is 2.96 Q_b, where Q_b is the output of your firm, at what output level should you operate to maximize profit?

b. What price should you charge?

c. How much will the industry as a whole produce at this price?

18. According to Franklin Fisher, Zvi Griliches, and Carl Kaysen, automobile model changes during the 1950's cost about $5 billion a year. Were these expenditures socially worthwhile? How can one tell?

19. According to the Senate Subcommittee on Antitrust and Monopoly, the ethical drug industry has had much higher profit rates, as a percent of net worth, than most other industries. Is this consistent with the predictions of the theory of oligopoly?

20. According to Milton Friedman, "Few trends could so thoroughly undermine the very foundations of our free society as the acceptance by corporate officials of a social responsibility other than to make as much money for their stockholders as possible." Do you agree? Why or why not?

21. In the early 1960's, a major aluminum firm raised its price for sheet by a penny a pound. Almost a month later, the increase was rescinded because the other aluminum producers did not go along with the increase. Is this consistent with the kinked oligopoly demand curve?

22. Joe Bain has estimated that the output of an efficient-sized fresh-meat-packing plant is at most 1 percent of industry sales. He has also estimated that the output of an efficient tractor manufacturing plant is equal to 10 to 15 percent of industry sales. Discuss the relevance of these facts for the market structure of these industries.

23. According to the Federal Trade Commission, there was collusion among the leading bakers and food outlets in the state of Washington in the late 1950's and early 1960's. Prior to the conspiracy, bread prices in Seattle were about equal to the U. S. average. During the period of the conspiracy, bread prices in Seattle were 15 to 20 percent above the U. S. average. Is this consistent with the theory of collusive behavior? Why do you think that bread prices in Seattle were not double or triple the U. S. average during the conspiracy?

24. According to John Stuart Mill, "where competitors are so few, they always agree not to compete. They may run a race of cheapness to ruin a new candidate, but as soon as he has established his footing, they come to terms with him." Do you agree or not? Why?

25. The following table shows, for food manufacturing, the relationship between the percentage of the industry output accounted for by the top four firms and the net profit on stockholder equity of firms in the industry.

Percentage held by top four firms	Net profit on stockholder equity (percentage)
31–40	6.2
41–49	9.2
50–59	12.9
60–69	14.6
70–90	16.3

Are these results what you would expect from the theory of oligopoly? Why or why not? (The data come from the Federal Trade Commission.)

Completion Questions

1. Under oligopoly, each firm is aware that its actions are likely to elicit _____ in the policies of its competitors.

2. A good example of oligopoly in the United States is the _____ industry.

3. If an oligopoly produces a homogeneous product, it is called a _____ oligopoly.

4. The Cournot model assumes that each firm thinks that the other will hold its output constant at _____.

5. The Edgeworth model assumes that each firm thinks that the other will hold its price ____ _____.

6. According to the Chamberlin model, the firms tacitly accept the _____ solution.

7. According to the kinked oligopoly demand curve, firms think that if they raise their price, their rivals will _____ .

8. According to the kinked oligopoly demand curve, firms think that if they lower their price, their rivals will _____ .

9. If a game is strictly determined, there is a _____ of each player.

10. Von Neumann and Morgenstern proved that a pair of optimal mixed strategies _____ _____ in a two-person zero-sum game.

True or False

_____ 1. Collusive agreements are legal in the United States.

_____ 2. Cartels are common and legally acceptable in Europe.

_____ 3. Cartels tend to be unstable because the demand curve facing a "cheater" is highly inelastic.

_____ 4. According to the dominant-firm model, the dominant firm allows the smaller firms to sell all they want at the price it sets.

_____ 5. Cost-plus pricing takes explicit account of the extent and elasticity of demand, as well as of marginal costs.

_____ 6. Whether or not an industry remains oligopolistic in the face of relatively easy entry depends on the size of the market for the product relative to the optimal size of firm.

_____ 7. There are very considerable barriers to entry in the steel, automobile, and aluminum industries.

_____ 8. A limit price is a price that is the maximum price the oligopolists can charge without courting the possibility of government antitrust action.

_____ 9. The basic purpose of advertising is to make the demand curve for the product more elastic.

_____ 10. Joe Bain has found that firms in industries in which the few largest firms had a high proportion of total sales tended to have higher profits than firms in industries in which the few largest firms had a small proportion of total sales.

Multiple Choice

1. If DD$'$ is the industry demand curve and marginal costs are zero, the Chamberlin model predicts that price will be
   a. OP$_0$
   b. OP$_1$
   c. OP$_2$

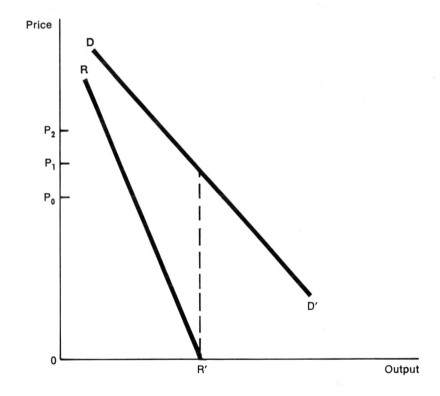

2. In the previous question, the RR$'$ curve is
   a. the marginal revenue curve.
   b. the marginal cost curve.
   c. the reaction curve.

3. A mixed strategy is a strategy where
   a. probabilities are assigned to pure strategies.
   b. a second-best approach is used.
   c. pure strategies are mixed with impure strategies.

4. In the following graph, which of the curves is a kinked oligopoly demand curve?
   a. AA$'$
   b. BB$'$
   c. CC$'$

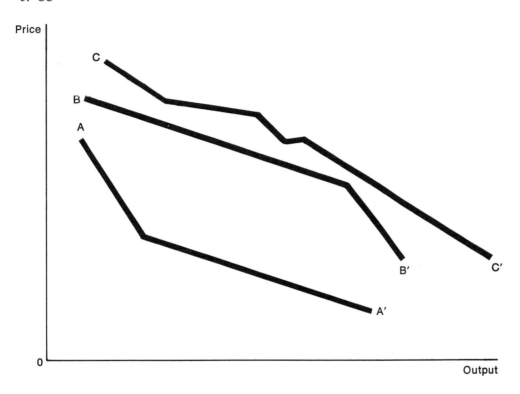

5. In the dominant-firm model, the dominant firm finds the demand curve for its output by
   a. using the unadjusted industry demand curve.
   b. adding up the small firms' demand curves.
   c. subtracting the small firms' supply from the industry demand curve.

CHAPTER 12 Price and Employment of Inputs under Perfect Competition

Key Concepts

Land
Labor
Capital
Rent
Wages
Profits
Firm's demand curve for an input
Value of marginal product
Market demand curve for an input

Derived demand
Price elasticity of demand for an input
Market supply curve for an input
Intermediate goods
Backward-bending supply curve
Quasi-rents
Qualitative differences in inputs
Wage differentials
Elasticity of substitution

Problems and Essays

1. Suppose that you own a car wash, and that its production function is

$$Q = -0.8 + 4.5L - .3L^2$$

where Q is the number of cars washed per hour and L is the number of men employed. Suppose that you receive $5 for each car washed and that the wage rate for each person you employ is $4.50. How many people should you employ to maximize profit? What will your profit amount to?

2. Suppose once again that you own the car wash described in the previous problem. How many people will you employ if the wage rate is \$1.50? How many if it is \$7.50? Based on these results, draw three points on your firm's demand curve for labor below.

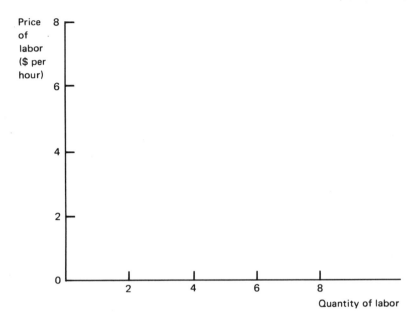

3. What factors determine the distribution of income? What role do input prices play?

4. Show that the cost-minimizing perfectly competitive firm will set

$$\frac{P_x}{MP_x} = \frac{P_y}{MP_y} = \cdots = \frac{P_z}{MP_z} = MC,$$

where P_x, P_y, and P_z are prices of inputs, MP_x, MP_y, and MP_z are marginal products of inputs, and MC is marginal cost.

5. Show that a profit-maximizing perfectly competitive firm will set an input's price equal to the value of its marginal product.

6. Suppose that labor is the only variable input, and that the marginal product of labor is as follows:

Amount of labor per year	Marginal product of labor
1	9
2	8
3	7
4	6
5	5
6	4

(Figures concerning the marginal product pertain to the interval between the indicated amount of labor and one unit less than this amount.) If the price of the product is $2 per unit and the firm is perfectly competitive, plot the firm's demand curve for labor in the graph below.

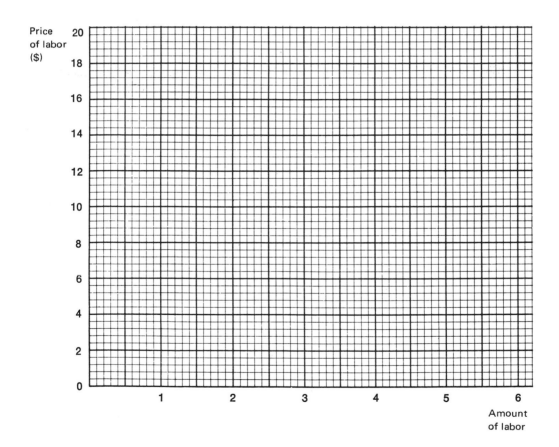

7. Describe and discuss the factors that influence the elasticity of demand for an input.

8. Describe the conditions that can result in a backward-bending supply curve for an input.

9. Why is a price of OP_0 not an equilibrium price? If OP_0 is the price, what forces will be set in motion to change it? Similarly, why is OP_1 not an equilibrium price? What is the equilibrium price for this input?

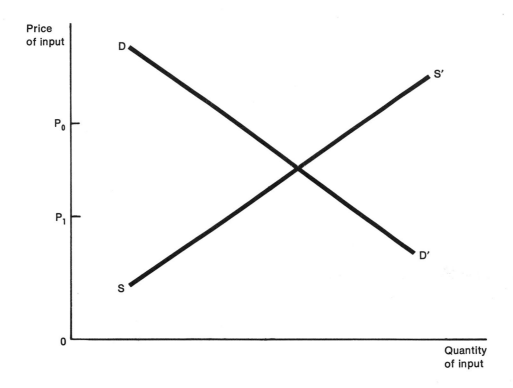

10. Show that a reduction of a payment to an input will not influence the availability and use of the input if the payment is a rent. Why is this important?

11. Describe what is meant by a quasi-rent.

12. Show that the differential in wages between skilled and unskilled plumbers should be equal to the differential in their marginal products.

13. Discuss some of the factors that could cause wage differentials even if labor were homogenous.

14. What is the elasticity of substitution? How is it related to the ratio of capital's total income to labor's total income?

15. (*Advanced*) Suppose that a textile plant's production function is $Q = L^{.8} K^{.2}$. If it takes the product price as given and the input prices as given, show that total wages paid by the firm will equal 80 percent of its revenues.

16. In the recent past, there was considerable concern expressed by government officials and others about the existence of an "oversupply" of certain kinds of scientists and engineers. Using the concepts developed by Kenneth Arrow and William Capron, analyze this situation and speculate concerning its causes.

17. Describe how Kenneth Arrow and William Capron used microeconomic theory to analyze the shortage of engineers and scientists in the 1950's.

18. Economists used microeconomic analysis to estimate the costs to the Department of Defense of an all-volunteer army. Can you guess how they went about doing this?

19. According to Elliot Berg, "the quantity of wage labor offered by the individual African tends to be inversely related to changes in village income and changes in wage rates." **What does this imply about the shape of the supply curve for labor? How do you explain this shape?**

20. Using the conventional supply and demand apparatus, show why black labor receives lower wages than white labor. What would happen to black wages, white wages, and total output if discrimination were to cease?

Completion Questions

1. If the ratio of each input's marginal product to its price is not the same for all inputs, the firm can _____ its costs by using some other input combination.

2. If a firm is maximizing profit under perfect competition, the ratio of the marginal product to the price of each input equals _____.

3. The value of the marginal product of an input equals the marginal product of the input times _____.

4. The price of an input in fixed supply is _____.

5. The elasticity of substitution measures the extent to which the ratio of capital to labor changes in response to changes in ____ _____

    _____.

6. If the elasticity of substitution is less than one, the effect of an increase in the price of labor relative to the price of capital is to _____ the ratio of capital's share (of total income) to labor's share (of total income).

7. A quasi-rent is paid to an input which is temporarily _____ in _____.

8. The price elasticity of demand for an input is generally greater in the _____ run than in the _____ run.

9. If an input's supply curve is backward-bending, beyond some point increases in its price bring forth _____ amounts supplied.

10. Wage differentials among labor of similar quality will arise to offset _____

_____ .

True or False

_____ 1. If more than one input is variable in quantity, the value-of-marginal-product curve will be the demand curve for an input.

_____ 2. Changes in the amounts used of other inputs will generally change the value-of-marginal-product curve for an input.

_____ 3. Under perfect competition, the supply of an input to an individual firm is perfectly inelastic.

_____ 4. Euler's theorem states that, if there are constant returns to scale, the total physical output of a firm will be identically equal to the sum of the amount of each input used multiplied by the input's marginal product.

_____ 5. Euler's theorem holds even if there are increasing returns to scale.

_____ 6. The more easily other inputs can be substituted for a certain input, the less price-elastic is the demand for this input.

_____ 7. In the case of a backward-bending supply curve for labor, the income effect more than offsets the substitution effect.

_____ 8. An intermediate good is a good that is produced neither by agriculture nor by manufacturing.

_____ 9. The price elasticity of demand by a firm for an input depends on the price elasticity of the good the firm produces.

_____ 10. Qualitative differences in inputs cannot be handled by microeconomic theory.

Multiple Choice

1. The traditional factors of production are:
   a. land and labor.
   b. land and capital.
   c. land, labor, and capital.

2. (*Advanced*) If one minimizes cost subject to the constraint that a certain output is produced, the Lagrange multiplier turns out to equal
   a. marginal revenue.
   b. average cost.
   c. marginal cost.

3. Kenneth Arrow and William Capron attribute the "shortage" of engineers and scientists in the 1950's to
   a. bad government planning.
   b. poor educational facilities.
   c. sticky prices.

4. The share of income going to labor in the United States has been
   a. declining markedly over time.
   b. relatively constant.
   c. subject to great variation.

5. The elasticity of substitution for the Cobb-Douglas production function is
   a. less than one.
   b. one.
   c. greater than one.

CHAPTER 13 Price and Employment of Inputs under Imperfect Competition

Key Concepts

Marginal revenue product
Firm's demand curve for an input
Market demand curve for an input
Market supply curve for an input
Monopsony
Oligopsony
Monopsonistic competition

Marginal expenditure curves
Labor unions
Collective bargaining
Bilateral monopoly
Union objectives
Economic effect of unions

Problems and Essays

1. According to Albert Rees, "A union will almost always insist on maintaining the current wage even at the cost of severe contraction in employemnt, whereas it would not insist on increasing the money wage if the consequences for employment were anything like as severe."* How can this fact be incorporated into our models of union behavior? What is the implication of this statement for classical theories of unemployment, which assumed that prices and wages are flexible?

*Albert Rees, *The Economics of Work and Pay*, New York: Harper and Row, 1973, p. 131.

2. Lloyd Reynolds has pointed out that the union sometimes presents demands that it does not expect to be acted on immediately. As he puts it, "It is the normal opening move in the chess game."* Give some examples of demands that were first met by outraged opposition by management, but which ultimately came to be accepted.

3. Describe how a profit-maximizing firm under imperfect competition will determine how much of each input to employ. Prove that this does indeed result in maximum profit.

*Lloyd Reynolds, *Labor Economics and Labor Relations,* Englewood Cliffs, N. J.: Prentice Hall, 1970, p. 435.

4. *a.* Suppose that a firm's demand curve for its product is as follows:

Output	Price of good
23	$5.00
32	4.00
40	3.50
47	3.00
53	2.00

Also, suppose that the marginal product and total product of labor is:

Amount of labor	Marginal product of labor	Total output
2	10	23
3	9	32
4	8	40
5	7	47
6	6	53

(Note that the figures regarding marginal product pertain to the interval between the indicated amount of labor and one unit less than the indicated amount of labor.) Given these data, how much labor would the firm employ if labor costs $12 a unit?

b. How much labor will the firm employ if labor costs $13 a unit?

c. How much labor will the firm employ if labor costs $10 a unit?

d. How much labor will the firm employ if labor costs $1 a unit?

e. Assuming labor is the only variable input, plot the firm's demand curve for labor in the graph below.

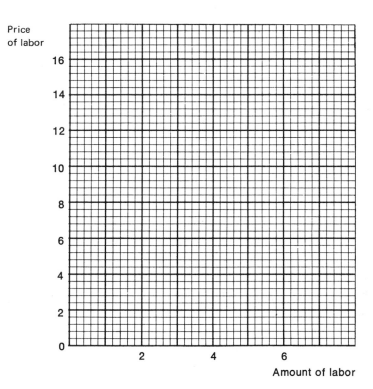

5. Prove that the marginal revenue product is the product of the marginal product and marginal revenue.

6. Discuss what is meant by monopsony. Give some cases in the real world where monopsony seems to be present.

7. If you were a laborer, would you prefer the labor market to be perfectly competitive or monopsonistic?

8. If you wanted your area to become a low-wage area, would you prefer the labor market to be perfectly competitive or monopsonistic? Why?

9. Describe the conditions determining how much of each input a profit-maximizing monopsonist will employ.

10. How can unions influence the wage rate paid to their members? Describe at least three ways that they can influence the wage.

11. Discuss the nature of union objectives. Give a few plausible kinds of union motivation and describe their implications for the wage rate and employment.

12. What do we know about the economic effects of unions? Describe the sorts of empirical studies that have been made, and summarize their results.

13. According to Ruth Greenslade, the ratio of average hourly earnings in the bituminous coal industry to that in general manufacturing rose from 1:1 at the turn of the century to about 2:1 at the peak of post-World War I union strength in the industry in 1922. Then as union strength declined in the industry, it declined to 1.07 in 1933. But as union strength increased subsequently, it increased too, and reached 1.7:1 in 1957. What do these findings seem to indicate about the economic effects of unionism?

14. Joseph Garbarino studied the behavior of wages in 34 manufacturing industries in 1923–40. He found that wages were directly related to degree of concentration of output, changes in output per man-hour, and extent of unionism. But the extent of unionism seemed least important and was not statistically significant. Comment on these findings.

15. According to Allan Cartter and F. Ray Marshall, the impact of unionism on wage levels of organized workers is most noticeable during periods of recession. Why?

16. According to Simon Rottenberg, in his discussion of the labor market for baseball players: "The reserve rule, which binds a player to the team that contracts him, gives a prima facie appearance of monopsony to the market."* Do you agree? What are the likely effects of this rule?

17. Allan Cartter and F. Ray Marshall state, "Reviewing the data from 1919 to the present, and particularly the last 15 years, there seems to be no indication that trade unions in general have increased labor's share of income."† How can one reconcile this finding with the feeling that unions in some industries have raised wages substantially?

*Simon Rottenberg, "The Baseball Players' Labor Market," *Journal of Political Economy,* June 1956.

†Allan Cartter and F. Ray Marshall, *Labor Economics,* Homewood, Ill.: Irwin, 1967.

Completion Questions

1. The condition for profit maximization under imperfect competition is that the firm should set the price of the input equal to _____ _____ .

2. The marginal revenue product of input differs from the value of the marginal product in the following way: _____ _____ .

3. If marginal revenue is equal to price, the marginal-revenue-product schedule becomes precisely the same as the _____ .

4. If all firms are monopolists in their product markets, the market demand curve for an input would simply be the _____ of the demand curves of the individual firms.

5. Monopsony is a case of _____ .

6. The classic case of monopsony is _____ _____ .

7. The marginal expenditure curve for an input lies _____ its supply curve.

8. If a monopsonist maximizes profit, he sets the marginal expenditure on an input equal to _____ .

9. The monopsonist employs _____ of the input than if the input market were perfectly competitive.

10. The monopsonist pays a _____ price for the input than if the input market were perfectly competitive.

True or False

_____ 1. Under perfect competition, the marginal expenditure for an input equals its price.

_____ 2. Organized baseball has some monopsonistic characteristics.

_____ 3. A monopsonist will hire inputs so that the ratio of the marginal product to the marginal expenditure for each input is the same for all inputs.

_____ 4. If a labor union tries to maximize its wage bill, it will try to operate at the point where its marginal revenue is zero.

_____ 5. In recent years, union wages have increased much more rapidly than nonunion wages.

_____ 6. The initial asking figure concerning wages put forth by a union in collective bargaining is likely to be lower than its real expectations.

_____ 7. The marginal-revenue-product curve for an input often has a positive slope.

_____ 8. The marginal revenue product of an input is equal to marginal revenue divided by marginal product.

_____ 9. Oligopsony occurs when there are few buyers.

_____ 10. The theory of bilateral monopoly, when applied to collective bargaining, assumes that the union wants to maximize the difference between the total wages that are paid to (employed) workers and the amount of money required to bring this amount of labor onto the market if each unit of labor were paid only the price necessary to induce it to work.

Multiple Choice

1. If the price of labor is $1 a unit, its marginal product is 2 tons of output, and the firm's marginal revenue is $5 per ton, the firm is
   a. minimizing cost.
   b. maximizing profit.
   c. not maximizing profit.

2. If there is only one variable input, the firm's demand curve for an input is obtained by multiplying
   a. marginal cost and marginal revenue curves.
   b. marginal product and marginal revenue curves.
   c. average cost and marginal revenue curves.

3. Under imperfect competition in the product market, the equilibrium price of an input is given by
   a. the intersection of the product demand and supply curves.
   b. the intersection of the input demand and supply curves.
   c. the intersection of the product demand and input supply curves.

4. Monopsony often stems from the fact that:
   a. an input is not mobile.
   b. an input is extremely mobile.
   c. an input is an intermediate good.

5. The marginal expenditure for an input will always be
   a. higher than the input's price.
   b. higher than the input's price if its supply curve is upward sloping.
   c. higher than the input's price if its supply curve is horizontal.

6. It makes perfectly good sense for a labor union to want to
   a. maximize the wage rate.
   b. maximize its marginal revenue.
   c. keep its members fully employed.

CHAPTER 14

General Equilibrium Analysis and Resource Allocation

Key Concepts

Partial equilibrium analysis
General equilibrium analysis
General equilibrium
Existence of general equilibrium
Uniqueness of general equilibrium
Numeraire
Input-output analysis
Input-output table

Production coefficients
Edgeworth box diagram
Exchange
Contract curve
Product transformation curve
Production and exchange in a two-
    good, two-consumer, two-input
    economy

The Allocation of a Scarce Resource: A Case for Discussion

About 1950, one of the key problems in the U.S. defense establishment was the allocation of fissionable material—U258 and Pu239. In particular, how much of our supply of fissionable material should be used for strategic purposes, and how much should be used for tactical purposes? The strategic forces, principally long-range bombers at that time, were the foundation of our capability to strike back at an enemy's cities and bases. The tactical forces were concerned with more limited engagements with enemy forces. At that time, the strategic mission had exclusive claim on the national stockpile of fissionable materials, and an urgent question was whether some tactical air squadrons should be equipped with small-yield atomic weapons. This very important question occupied and concerned the minds of some of the nation's highest officials.

Both for the strategic and tactical mission, the two most important determinants of the effectiveness of the mission were (1) the amount of fissionable material used, and (2) the number of aircraft used. Within limits, it was possible to substitute airplanes for fissionable material and vice versa. For example, if the object of an Air Force operation was the expected destruction of a certain number of targets, fewer aircraft would be required to destroy these targets if atomic weapons, rather than conventional weapons, were used. Also, one way of increasing the probability that a bomb would get to the target was to have several empty decoy bombers accompanying each aircraft with an atomic bomb, which clearly was a way of substituting aircraft for fissionable materials.

In the very short run, it was sensible to view the total number of aircraft available for either strategic or tactical missions as fixed. It was also sensible to view the total amount of fissionable material available for either strategic or tactical missions as fixed. (However, this was appropriate only in analyzing the problem in the short run; in the long run, it was possible to add to our supplies of aircraft and fissionable materials.) Also, it is important to note that there was no way to establish the relative importance of strategic and tactical targets. For example, no one was willing to say that the destruction of a strategic target was worth the destruction of two tactical targets. Instead, strategic and tactical targets were regarded as incommensurable.*

Show how the simple principles of welfare economics can enable you to solve this problem. (In fact, this problem was solved by the application of the simple principles described in Chapter 14.)

Problems and Essays

1. According to Robert Dorfman, Paul Samuelson, and Robert Solow, input-output analysis "rejects as unrealistic the Austrian economists' view that you can identify certain industries as being in 'earlier' stages of production and certain other industries as being in 'later' stages."† What do they mean? Do you agree? Why or why not?

---

*Consequently, it was not possible to combine the expected number of strategic and tactical targets destroyed into a single measure of destructive impact and solve the problem by finding the allocation of aircraft and fissionable material that maximized this overall measure of destructive impact.

†R. Dorfman, P. Samuelson, and R. Solow, *Linear Programming and Economic Analysis,* New York: McGraw-Hill, 1958, p. 205.

2. Robert Dorfman, Paul Samuelson, and Robert Solow point out that "a system which leaves many supply and demand functions (or the utility and production functions which lie one step further back) almost completely unspecified as to shape can yield only incomplete results."* Explain the significance of this fact for general equilibrium analysis.

3. What is general equilibrium analysis? How does it differ from partial equilibrium analysis?

Ibid., p. 349.

4. When should one use general equilibrium analysis? When should one use partial equilibrium analysis?

5. Define a state of general equilibrium. Can we be sure that a state of general equilibrium can be achieved?

6. Describe the conditions given by Kenneth Arrow and Gerard Debreu that are sufficient for the existence of general equilibrium. Are these conditions necessary for its existence?

7. Construct a simple general equilibrium model. Count up the number of equations and the number of variables.

8. Describe the nature and purposes of input-output analysis. Be sure to specify its key assumptions.

9. *a.* Suppose that the following table shows the amount of each type of input used per dollar of output:

Type of input	Output		
	Electric power	*Coal*	*Chemicals*
Electric Power	$0.1	$0.3	$0.0
Coal	0.5	0.1	0.0
Chemicals	0.2	0.0	0.9
Labor	0.2	0.6	0.1
TOTAL	1.0	1.0	1.0

Express the value of electric power output as a function of the value of coal output and the value of chemical output.

b. Express the value of coal output as a function of the value of the output of other goods.

c. Express the value of chemical output as a function of the value of the output of other goods.

d. Suppose that this economy has set production targets of $100 million of electric power, $50 million of coal, and $50 million of chemicals. How much electric power must be produced?

e. Given these targets, how much coal must be produced?

f. Given these targets, how much chemicals must be produced?

g. Given these targets, how much labor must be used?

10. What factors might cause changes over time in the technical coefficients in input-output analysis?

11. How can one derive the contract curve in an Edgeworth box diagram representing exchange between two consumers? What is the significance of the contract curve?

12. Describe how a product transformation curve can be derived from an Edgeworth box diagram representing production of two goods.

13. Given the amount of each commodity to be produced, how should this output be allocated and how should inputs be allocated in the two-good, two-input, two-consumer case?

14. Describe how input-output analysis might be used to analyze the effects of disarmament on the American economy.

15. Describe how input-output analysis might be of use to an economist interested in forecasting the sales of the U. S. Steel Corporation next year.

16. According to an input-output table prepared by the Bureau of Labor Statistics for 1947, the chemical industry produced $14 billion of output.* This table also shows that the biggest purchaser of this output is the chemical industry. How can this be? Isn't there a contradiction here?

17. Werner Hirsch[†] constructed an input-output model that included local government as an "industry." How would you go about doing this? What sorts of problems are there in this approach?

*Wassily Leontief, "Input-Output Economics," *Scientific American*, October 1951.
†Werner Hirsch, "Input-Output Techniques for Urban Government Decisions," *American Economic Review*, May 1968.

Completion Questions

1. Partial equilibrium analysis is adequate in cases where the effect of a change in market conditions in one market has _____ repercussion on prices in other markets.

2. _____ is the branch of microeconomics that deals with the interrelations among various decision-making units and various markets.

3. A state of _____ can be achieved under a wide set of circumstances in a _____ economy.

4. _____ puts general equilibrium analysis in a form that is operationally useful.

5. Input-output analysis emphasizes the _____ of the economic system.

6. Wassily Leontief, the founder of _____ , assumes that production coefficients are _____ .

7. It is impossible for a combination of outputs lying outside the _____ to be produced.

8. If we connect the points of tangency of one person's indifference curves with the other person's indifference curves in an Edgeworth box diagram, we obtain the _____ _____ .

9. Consumer satisfaction will not be maximized unless the marginal rate of product transformation between two goods is equal to the _____ _____ .

10. The contract curve is an optimal set of points in the sense that, if the consumers are off the contract curve, it is always preferable for them to _____ _____ .

True or False

_____ 1. There is only one set of absolute prices that results in general equilibrium.

_____ 2. It is very difficult to find reasonable conditions under which a perfectly competitive economy is in a state of general equilibrium.

_____ 3. The complexity of input-output models is not substantially increased if the assumption of fixed production coefficient is relaxed.

_____ 4. If commodities are allocated optimally, the marginal rate of substitution between a pair of commodities must be the same for all consumers that consume both.

_____ 5. If commodities are allocated optimally, the marginal rate of substitution between any pair of commodities must be the same for all pairs of commodities.

_____ 6. In the case of production, it is not optimal for producers to move to a point on the contract curve.

_____ 7. A point that is inside the product transformation curve is an efficient point.

_____ 8. Input-output analysis involves the solution of a number of simultaneous linear equations.

_____ 9. Changes in the relative prices of inputs may result in changes in production coefficients.

_____ 10. A product transformation curve often has a positive slope.

Multiple Choice

1. No market can adjust to a change in conditions without
   a. a change in other markets.
   b. other markets remaining unchanged.
   c. governmental aid.

2. General equilibrium analysis is required in
   a. some cases.
   b. all cases.
   c. only those cases where the auto industry is included.

3. Whether or not there is a solution to a set of equations can
   a. never be determined by comparing the number of variables with the number of equations.
   b. always be determined by comparing the number of variables with the number of equations.
   c. under certain circumstances be determined by comparing the number of variables with the number of equations.

4. Input-output analysis has been used to
   a. analyze problems of defense and mobilization.
   b. determine the relationship of imports and exports to domestic production.
   c. analyze problems of underdeveloped countries.
   d. all of the above.

5. Compared with a certain point on the contract curve, a point off the contract curve
    a. may be better.
    b. is certainly better.
    c. is never better.

6. If a point is off the contract curve, we can find
    a. a point on the contract curve that is better.
    b. no point on the contract curve that is better.
    c. a point on the contract curve that is better, if and only if the contract curve is a circle.

CHAPTER 15 Welfare Economics

Key Concepts

Welfare economics
Interpersonal comparison of utility
Distribution of income
Marginal conditions for optimal
   resource allocation
Utility-possibility curve
Social welfare function
Marginal cost pricing
External economies of production
External diseconomies of production

External economies of consumption
External diseconomies of consumption
Public goods
Pareto criterion
Kaldor criterion
Scitovsky criterion
Bergson criterion
Arrow's impossibility theorem
Theory of the second best

Problems and Essays

1. William Baumol has pointed out that the cafes in the Piazza San Marco in Venice "hire bands to serenade their customers. But, being outdoors, they cannot avoid providing music to the patrons of adjoining bistros. Unfortunately, however, with four or five of these going at once it becomes impossible to hear the music anywhere."* Analyze this situation, using the concepts of external economies and diseconomies.

*W. Baumol, *Economic Theory and Operations Analysis,* Englewood Cliffs, N.J.: Prentice Hall, 1965, p. 370.

2. According to William Baumol, "the idea of external economies and diseconomies has taught us to beware of policies which yield optimal results for each of the various divisions of a firm taken by themselves."* What is so dangerous about such policies? Suppose that you were hired by a large corporation to write a report on the pitfalls involved in such policies. What points would you stress?

3. Discuss the difficulties involved in making interpersonal comparisons of utility. Is it possible at all? What implications does this have for objective analysis of the optimal distribution of income?

*Ibid., p. 384.

4. State the three necessary marginal conditions for optimal resource allocation. Are these conditions sufficient as well as necessary for optimality?

5. Suppose that I regard an extra unit of peanut butter as having the same utility as 2 extra units of jelly, but you regard an extra unit of peanut butter as having the same utility as 3 extra units of jelly. Is this an optimal situation? If not, how can it be improved?

6. If the marginal rate of technical substitution between labor and capital is not the same for two producers, show how output can be increased by reallocating labor and capital.

7. Prove that, for optimal resource allocation, the marginal rate of substitution between any two commodities must be the same as the marginal rate of transformation between these two commodities for any producer.

8. Show that, if marginal cost varies from firm to firm, industry output must be produced inefficiently. Relate this fact to agricultural price supports.

9. Show how one can derive a utility-possibility curve in the two-commodity, two-input, two-consumer case.

10. What is a social welfare function? Show how a social welfare function, coupled with the utility-possibility curve, can enable us to get a complete solution to the two-commodity, two-input, two-consumer case.

11. Can we be sure that the three necessary conditions for welfare maximization are satisfied under perfect competition? Are they satisfied under monopoly?

12. Discuss the advantages of marginal cost pricing.

13. According to Thomas Marschak, marginal cost pricing has resulted in savings in the French nationalized electricity industry. For example, he states that there seems to have been a leveling of consumption between the daytime and nighttime periods. Why do you think this occurred?

14. Discuss the meaning and importance of external economies and diseconomies, both of consumption and production. How do they alter the optimality of perfect competition?

15. Indicate how the theory of external economies and diseconomies sheds light on public policy toward basic research.

16. What is a public good? Will perfect competition result in an optimal allocation of such goods?

17. Describe Arrow's impossibility theorem and its significance.

18. Describe the theory of the second best and its significance.

19. According to William Vickrey, "By far the most important of the considerations that conflict with the strict application of marginal cost pricing is the need for revenues." Why is this the case? How can one get around this difficulty?

20. According to Milton Friedman,* significant external economies are gained from the education of children: "The gain from the education of a child accrues not only to the child or its parents but also to other members of the society." Moreover, "it is not feasible to identify the particular individuals (or families) benefited and so to charge for the services rendered." What kind of government action is justified by these considerations?

21. Milton Friedman† states, "One argument frequently made for public housing is based on an alleged neighborhood effect: slum districts in particular, and low quality housing to a lesser degree, are said to impose higher costs on the community in the form of fire and police protection. This literal neighborhood effect may well exist. But insofar as it does, it alone argues, not for public housing, but for higher taxes on the kind of housing that adds to social costs since this would tend to equalize private and social cost." Comment on this statement.

*Milton Friedman, *Capitalism and Freedom*, Chicago, University of Chicago Press, 1962.
†*Ibid.*

22. According to Ronald Coase, "Analysis in terms of divergencies between private and social products concentrates attention on particular deficiencies in the system and tends to nourish the belief that any measure which will remove the deficiency is necessarily desirable. It diverts attention from those other changes in the system which are inevitably associated with the corrective measure, changes which may well produce more harm than the original deficiency."* Do you agree? Comment on this statement.

23. According to a study done by Jack Hirshleifer, James De Haven, and Jerome Milliman, water rights sometimes cannot be freely traded in the United States. What effect will this have on the efficiency of the allocation of water supplies?

*Ronald Coase, "The Problem of Social Cost," reprinted in Edwin Mansfield, *Microeconomics: Selected Readings*, 2d ed., New York: Norton, 1975.

24. Hirshleifer, De Haven, and Milliman state that in some cities (for example, Los Angeles) the price of water is lower for some water uses—irrigation, for example—than for others. What effect does this have on the efficiency of the allocation of water supplies?

Completion Questions

1. There is _____ on which we can validly measure pleasure or pain so that inter-personal comparisons can validly be made.

2. Whether or not one income distribution is better than another is a _____

    _____.

3. The marginal conditions for optimal resource allocation imply that consumers are on their

    _____.

4. The marginal conditions for optimal resource allocation imply that producers are on their

    _____.

5. If there were only one consumer, the marginal conditions for optimal resource allocation would imply that his indifference curve be tangent to the _____

    _____.

6. Under perfect competition, the marginal rate of substitution between two goods is the same for any pair of consumers because they pay _____ for the goods.

7. Under perfect competition, the marginal rate of technical substitution between two inputs is the same for any pair of producers because they pay _____ _____ for the inputs.

8. A firm that is polluting a stream without incurring any cost is an example of an _____

    _____.

9. When one firm benefits from another firm's research, this is an example of an _____

    _____.

10. National defense and a lighthouse are examples of _____ goods.

True or False

_____ 1. According to the Pareto criterion, a change that harms no one and improves the lot of at least one person is an improvement.

_____ 2. According to the Pareto criterion, a dollar taken from a rich man and given to a poor man is an improvement.

_____ 3. Kaldor's criterion does not require that compensation actually be paid by the gainers to the losers.

_____ 4. Under certain circumstances, the Kaldor criterion will indicate that a change is an improvement, but it will also indicate that a change back to the original state of affairs is an improvement.

_____ 5. Bergson's criterion does away with any reliance on a social welfare function.

_____ 6. Kenneth Arrow's impossibility theorem showed that it was impossible to escape dictatorship if society's allocation of resources was to be efficient.

_____ 7. The attainment of a Pareto optimum does not require the fulfillment of all of the marginal conditions for optimal resource allocation.

_____ 8. The theory of the second best implies that the reduction of the number of monopolies in the economy from 12 to 8 may not be a good thing.

_____ 9. A social welfare function can rather easily be estimated for the United States by fitting curves to historical data.

_____ 10. Perfect competition results in an optimal allocation of resources. Public goods will be allocated the right amount of resources without government intervention or other nonmarket mechanisms.

Multiple Choice

1. Suppose that the product transformation curve looks as in the diagram below:
   This is due to
   a. decreasing returns.
   b. external economies.
   c. increasing returns.

2. Scitovsky's criterion is intended to meet a weakness in
   a. the Bergson criterion.
   b. the Kaldor criterion.
   c. the Pareto criterion.

3. The marginal conditions for optimal resource allocation
   a. depend on interpersonal comparisons of utility.
   b. help to determine the optimal distribution of income.
   c. are silent concerning the optimal distribution of income.

4. Marginal cost pricing is automatically the rule under
   a. monopoly.
   b. oligopoly.
   c. monopolistic competition.
   d. perfect competition.

5. If a perfectly competitive industry is monopolized, the result is that
   a. the marginal conditions for optimal resource allocation are no longer fulfilled.
   b. the marginal conditions for optimal resource allocation are still fulfilled.
   c. more of the marginal conditions for optimal resource allocation are fulfilled than was formerly the case.

6. The theory of the second best shows that piecemeal attempts to fulfill the marginal conditions for optimal resource allocation
   a. are bound to be worthwhile.
   b. can easily be a mistake.
   c. are always a mistake.

CHAPTER 16 Technological Change and Economic Progress

Key Concepts

Technology

Technological change

Change in technique

Capital-saving technological change

Labor-saving technological changes

Neutral technological change

Capital-embodied technological change

Disembodied technological change

Productivity growth

Total productivity index

Research and development

Learning

Parallel development efforts

Time-cost tradeoffs

Innovation

Diffusion of innovations

Static efficiency

Economic progress

Patent system

Problems and Essays

1. According to F. M. Scherer, "Some of the most blatant price fixing schemes in American economic history were erected on a foundation of agreements to cross-license complementary and competing patents."* How could such schemes come about? What were some of the industries where such schemes occurred?

*F. M. Scherer, *Industrial Market Structure and Economic Performance*, Skokie, Ill.: Rand McNally, 1970, p. 392–93.

2. In recent years, there has been a great deal of concern over the acquisition of coal firms by petroleum firms. Four of the nation's ten biggest coal companies—Pittsburgh and Midway, Consolidation, Island Creek, and Old Ben—were acquired by oil firms in the 1960's. What effect do you think this will have on the rate of technological change in coal?

3. Define technological change. In principle, how can certain types of technological change be measured? Can this technique deal with new products?

4. What is the difference between a change in technique and technological change? Can the former occur without the latter? Can the latter occur without the former?

5. Describe what is meant by capital-saving technological change, labor-saving technological change, and neutral technological change. Show how the isoquants shift in each case.

6. What is the difference between capital-embodied and disembodied technological change? Give some examples of each type of technological change.

7. Is the growth of output per man-hour a complete measure of the rate of technological change? If not, why not? Is it commonly used for this purpose?

8. What is the total productivity index? What advantages does it have over output per man-hour? Under what circumstances is it precisely the proper measure of the rate of technological change?

9. What are some of the difficulties in practically all indirect estimates of the rate of technological change based on "residuals" or unexplained productivity change?

10. What are some of the principal determinants of the rate of technological change in a particular industry?

11. What is research and development? In what sense is R and D a learning process?

12. Under what circumstances does it make sense to use parallel development efforts?

13. What determines how much a particular development project will cost?

14. What is meant by an innovation? How does it differ from an invention? Is there commonly a long lag between invention and innovation? Why is innovation economically important?

15. What determines how rapidly the use of an innovation spreads?

16. Summarize the arguments of J. K. Galbraith and Joseph Schumpeter to the effect that imperfect competition stimulates economic progress. Also summarize the arguments of their critics.

17. Does the evidence indicate that an industry dominated by a few giant firms is generally more progressive than one composed of a larger number of smaller firms? Summarize the evidence.

18. Describe the disadvantages of the patent system from the viewpoint of static efficiency.

19. According to John Kendrick, output per unit of labor input increased by 5.1 percent per year in the tobacco industry during 1899–1953 and by 3.5 percent per year in the chemical industry during 1899–1953. The chemical industry spends much more on research and development than does the tobacco industry. Does this mean that R and D has relatively little impact on an industry's rate of technological change?

20. The annual rate of increase of the total productivity index during 1899–1953 was 3.5 percent in the transportation equipment industry and 1.6 percent in the beverage industry. What sorts of factors may be able to explain this difference?

21. Figures provided by the Bureau of Labor Statistics show that output per man-hour in blast furnaces using the most up-to-date techniques was about twice as large as the industry average in 1926. How can such large differences exist at a given point in time? Why don't all firms adopt the most up-to-date techniques at every point in time?

22. According to John Enos, about nine years passed between the time when catalytic cracking was invented by Eugene Houdry and the time when it was first introduced commercially. What factors may be able to account for this long lag?

23. According to Robert Solow, "Invention is the historical answer to the law of diminishing returns." Explain this statement.

24. Data gathered by the National Science Foundation show that in 1961, drug firms employing 5000 or more people spent 4.4 percent of sales on research and development, while drug firms employing 1000–4999 people spent 5.8 percent of sales on research and development. Do these data concerning the drug industry support John Kenneth Galbraith's thesis concerning the technical progressiveness of giant firms?

Completion Questions

1. Technology is _____ regarding the industrial arts.

2. Technological change results in a _____ in the production function.

3. If there are _____, there is at a given point in time a unique relationship between capital input per unit of output and labor input per unit of output.

4. If technological change results in a greater percentage reduction in capital input than labor input, it is _____.

5. Technological change is _____ if the marginal rate of technical substitution of labor for capital diminishes.

6. The total productivity index is _____.

7. A research and development project can be regarded as a process of _____ _____ reduction.

8. As the prospective amount of learning increases and the cost of running each effort decreases, the optimal number of parallel development efforts _____.

9. An invention, when applied for the first time, is called an _____ _____.

10. The lag between invention and innovation is commonly _____ years or more for major inventions.

True or False

_____ 1. A firm almost never is wise to wait more than a few weeks in introducing an innovation.

_____ 2. Learning takes place among the users of an innovation but not among the producers of an innovation.

_____ 3. The probability that a firm not using an innovation will adopt it in the next few months is independent of the proportion of the firms in the industry already using it.

_____ 4. The rate of diffusion of an innovation is greater for more profitable innovations than for less profitable ones.

_____ 5. The marginal conditions for optimal resource allocation in Chapter 15 assume that the level of technology is fixed.

_____ 6. If an imperfectly competitive economy has a higher rate of technological change and productivity growth, this may offset its static inefficiency.

_____ 7. Practically all economists agree that an economy composed of monopolies would have the highest rate of technological change and productivity growth.

_____ 8. The available evidence indicates that an industry dominated by a few giant firms is always more progressive than one composed of a large number of smaller firms.

_____ 9. The patent system has the disadvantage that new knowledge is not used as widely as it should be from the viewpoint of static efficiency.

_____ 10. The patent system results in marginal-cost pricing for new information.

Multiple Choice

1. All changes in technique
   a. result from technological change.
   b. result from changes in input prices.
   c. mean that a change occurs in utilized methods of production.

2. If the marginal rate of technical substitution of labor for capital increases (holding the capital-labor ratio constant), technological change is
   a. labor-saving.
   b. capital-saving.
   c. neutral.

3. The diesel locomotive was an example of
   a. disembodied technological change.
   b. capital-embodied technological change.
   c. cost-increasing technological change.

4. The growth of output per man-hour is
   a. an adequate measure of the rate of technological change.
   b. influenced by the rate of technological change.
   c. independent of the rate of technological change.

5. The rate of technological change is influenced by
   a. demand factors only.
   b. supply factors only.
   c. both demand and supply factors.

6. The Schumpeter-Galbraith hypothesis
   a. is wrong in its entirety.
   b. is right in saying that a perfectly competitive industry would be unlikely to be able to carry out the R and D required for a high rate of technological change in some parts of the economy.
   c. is right in saying that an industry composed of a very few giant firms is the best market structure from the point of view of promoting technological change and rapid acceptance of innovations.

CHAPTER 17 Public Goods, Benefit-Cost Analysis, and Environmental Protection

Key Concepts

Public good
Exclusion principle
Rivalry in consumption
Benefit-cost analysis
Real benefits
Pecuniary benefits

Air pollution
Water pollution
Thermal pollution
Direct regulation
Effluent fee

Problems and Essays

1. What is the exclusion principle? Does this principle hold for private goods? For public goods?

2. What is meant by rivalry in consumption? Is this characteristic found among private goods? Public goods?

3. Why is it that people often fail to reveal their true preferences concerning public goods?

4. Do you sum individual demand curves vertically or horizontally to get the market demand curve for a *private* good? Why?

5. Do you sum individual demand curves vertically or horizontally to get the market demand curve for a *public* good? Why?

6. Suppose that the Department of Transportation has a budget of $10 million to spend on roads, and that the costs and benefits from all proposed roads are as follows:

Road	Benefits	Costs
X to Y	$20 million	$10 million
X to Z	5 million	3 million
Y to Z	6 million	7 million

How should the department spend its $10 million? Why?

7. In question 6, suppose that the Office of Management and Budget says that the Department of Transportation can spend all that it wants (up to $20 million) on roads. Which roads should the department build? Why?

8. According to Roland McKean, "It is in connection with comparatively narrow problems of choice that cost-benefit analysis can sometimes play a more significant role." What does he mean? Do you agree? Why or why not?

9. According to A. R. Prest and Ralph Turvey, savings of time by drivers and passengers "often form a very high proportion of total estimated benefits of road improvements. . . . Unfortunately, [estimates of the value of these savings]. . . have not so far been very satisfactory." How would you go about making such estimates? What problems would you encounter? How accurate do you think your results would be?

10. A. R. Prest and Ralph Turvey point out that the benefit-cost ratio for a cross-Florida barge canal was estimated to be 1.20 by the Corps of Engineers, but only 0.13 by some consultants retained by the railroads. What factors might account for the difference in these results?

11. On the basis of the benefit-cost analyses carried out by the Department of the Interior and the Federal Power Commission, would you be in favor of building a dam on the Middle Snake river? Why or why not?

12. What are the basic causes of environmental pollution in our society?

13. What is an effluent fee? How can it be used to reduce pollution to more satisfactory levels? Have effluent fees been used elsewhere?

14. The Environmental Protection Agency has pointed out that a fundamental problem is, "At what point do the additional costs of controlling all sources of pollutants exceed the additional benefits of improved water quality?" EPA responds to this question by saying, "Clearly the current societal concern for environmental quality indicates that the public believes that there are significant benefits yet to be attained."* Do you agree? Do you think that this answers the question? How can the question be answered?

15. The 1972 Amendments to the Federal Water Pollution Control Act require industries to use "best practicable" water pollution control technology by mid-1977 and "best available" technology by mid-1983. Do you think that this is proper public policy? Why or why not?

*The Economics of Clean Water, EPA, 1973, p. 8

16. According to EPA, "individual plants in certain industries will experience difficulties in meeting the requirements."* Why? In what industries would you expect the difficulties to be greatest? What kinds of firms will be most affected?

17. Should a person living in the Mojave Desert take the same pains to reduce air pollution as someone living in Pasadena? According to Larry Ruff, California law makes no distinction between these situations.† Should it?

---

*The Economics of Clean Water, EPA, 1973, p. 6

†L. Ruff, "The Economic Common Sense of Pollution," reprinted in E. Mansfield, *Microeconomics: Selected Readings*, 2d ed., New York: Norton, 1975.

18. Some people ask, "If we can go to the moon, why can't we eliminate pollution?" How would you answer this question?

Completion Questions

1. A "free rider" is _____ .

2. The demand curve for a _____ good will not be revealed.

3. If the total budget is fixed, projects should be chosen that have the highest

   _____ ratios.

4. If the total budget is not fixed, projects should be chosen where the

   _____ ratio exceeds _____ .

5. If projects are divisible, a government agency should allocate funds so that the

   _____ from an extra dollar of expenditure on each project equals

   the _____ from an extra dollar of expenditure in the private sector.

6. _____ benefits and costs arise because of changes in relative prices.

7. Marginal social cost equals marginal _____ cost plus marginal

   _____ cost.

8. The more an industry cuts down on the amount of wastes it discharges, the

   _____ are its costs of pollution control.

9. The more untreated waste an industry dumps into the environment, the _____
   the cost of pollution.

10. The optimal level of pollution is generally not _____ .

11. An _____ is a fee that a polluter must pay to the government for discharging waste.

12. _____ have been used successfully in the Ruhr Valley.

True or False

_____ 1. Public goods will be provided in the right amount by the market mechanism.

_____ 2. Goods where there is rivalry in consumption are called public goods.

_____ 3. An uncrowded bridge is an example of a public good.

_____ 4. National defense is not a public good.

_____ 5. For a public good, the market demand curve is the horizontal summation of the individual demand curves.

_____ 6. Benefit-cost analysis has been used only in the past ten years.

_____ 7. Pecuniary benefits do not influence the distribution of income.

_____ 8. The Department of the Interior's study of the Middle Snake hydroelectric project was accepted by the staff of the Federal Power Commission.

_____ 9. In large part, environmental pollution is due to external economies.

_____ 10. The price paid by polluters for water and air is often less than the true social costs.

_____ 11. Pollution is tied inextricably to national output.

_____ 12. The only way to reduce pollution is to reduce population.

Multiple Choice

1. Technological change
   a. has made people more interdependent.
   b. has brought about more and stronger external diseconomies.
   c. has resulted in some harmful ecological changes.
   d. is a powerful positive force in the fight against pollution.
   e. all of the above.

2. If SS' shows the marginal social cost of a product and DD' is the product's demand curve, the optimal output of the product is
   a. less than 500.
   b. 500.
   c. 600.
   d. more than 600.

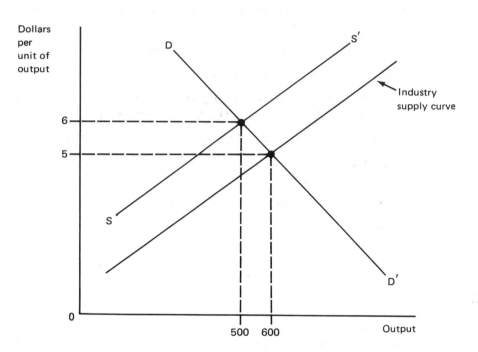

3. In the previous problem, the market mechanism, left to its own devices, would result in an output of
   a. less than 500.
   b. 500.
   c. 600.
   d. more than 600.

4. Continuing the previous problem, at the output that would result from the market mechanism, the marginal social cost of the product would be _____ its marginal social value.
   a. greater than
   b. equal to
   c. less than

5. In general, there is _____ between an industry's output and the amount of pollution it generates.
   a. a proportional relationship
   b. no fixed or proportional relationship
   c. no relationship whatsoever

6. To reduce pollution, the government can
   a. institute effluent fees.
   b. enact direct regulations.
   c. both a and b.

7. Economists tend to prefer effluent fees over direct regulation because such fees are more likely to
   a. achieve a reduction in pollution more cheaply.
   b. require less information on the part of government agencies.
   c. both a and b.

Answers

CHAPTER 1

Problems and Essays

1. He meant that a monopolist, having succeeded in freeing himself from competition, is likely to take things easy, and worry less about efficiency.
2. No. No. They must provide information that is useful in predicting the characteristics of the final airplane.
3. It helps to indicate how firms should analyze their production, marketing, and financial problems in order to increase their profitability.
4. Economics is concerned with the way in which resources are allocated among alternative uses to satisfy human wants. Microeconomics deals with the economic behavior of individual units like consumers, firms, and resource owners; macroeconomics deals with the behavior of economic aggregates like gross national product and the level of employment.
5. Business firms are constantly faced with the problem of choosing among alternative ways of producing their product. One type of problem that microeconomics can help to solve is: which technique will maximize the firm's profits?

   Firms are also faced with the problem of pricing their product. Another type of problem that microeconomics can help to solve is: which price will maximize the firm's profits?

   Society as a whole must decide how it wants to organize the production and distribution of goods and services. Microeconomics can sometimes be useful in helping to indicate what changes society would be justified in making in this system.

   Public policy must also be concerned with the structure of individual markets and industries. Microeconomics plays an important role in helping to illuminate antitrust cases and to solve problems in this area.
6. No.

   Why is steak more expensive than hamburger? Why are physicians paid more than carpenters? How will an increase in the price of margarine affect the amount of butter purchased by Mrs. Smith? Why are there so many producers of wheat and so few producers of automobiles?

   Pure mathematics is not concerned with the solution of particular problems, but it has turned out that various branches of mathematics are of great value in solving practical problems. This is true as well of much of microeconomic theory. Also, microeconomics, like mathematics, is extremely important as a basis for understanding the world around us and for further professional training.
7. Human wants are the things, services, goods, and circumstances that people desire.

   Human wants—or, more precisely, their fulfillment—are the objective at which economic activity is directed.
8. Resources are the things or services used to produce goods which can be used to satisfy wants. Economic resources are scarce, and thus have a nonzero price.

   The essence of "the economic problem" is that some resources are scarce and must be allocated among alternative uses. If all resources were free, there would be no economic problem.
9. Land is a shorthand expression for natural resources.
   Labor is human effort, both physical and mental.
   Capital includes equipment, buildings, inventories, raw materials, and other nonhuman producible resources.
10. Technology is society's pool of knowledge regarding the industrial arts.

Yes. Pure science is directed toward understanding, whereas technology is directed toward use.

Technology sets limits on the amount and type of goods that can be derived from a given amount of resources.

11. First, an economic system must allocate its resources among competing uses and combine these resources to produce the desired output efficiently.

Second, an economic system must determine the level and composition of output.

Third, an economic system must determine how the goods and services that are produced are distributed among the members of society.

Fourth, an economic system must provide for an adequate rate of growth of per capita income.

12. Consumers choose the amount of each good that they want, and producers act in accord with these decisions. Also, the production of some goods is a matter of political decision.

13. The price system is used to indicate the desires of workers and the relative value of various types of materials and equipment as well as the desires of consumers. To firms, profits are the carrot and losses are the stick. In addition, the government intervenes directly in some areas like weapons acquisition.

14. The income of an individual depends largely on the quantities of resources of various kinds that he owns and the prices he gets for them. In addition, the government modifies the resulting distribution of income by imposing progressive income taxes and by welfare programs like aid to dependent children.

15. The rate at which labor and capital resources are increased is motivated, at least in part, through the price system. Increases in efficiency, due in considerable measure to the advance of technology, are also stimulated by the price system. But the government plays an extremely significant role in supporting research and development.

16. A model is composed of a number of assumptions from which conclusions—or predictions—are drawn.

No.

The real world is so complex that it is necessary to simplify and abstract if any progress is to be made. A model may be the cheapest way of obtaining needed information.

17. The most important test of a model is how well it predicts. Another is whether its assumptions are logically consistent. Another important consideration is the range of phenomena to which the model applies.

18. No.

No.

Yes, according to a consensus of the economics profession.

Completion Questions

1. resources; human wants
2. individual consumers, firms, and resource owners
3. vary
4. goods and services
5. free
6. capital
7. use; understanding
8. consumers; producers
9. the price of each resource
10. rate of increase of the efficiency with which they are used

True or False

1. True 2. True 3. False 4. False 5. False 6. False 7. False 8. False 9. False 10. True

Multiple Choice

1. *c* 2. *e* 3. *c* 4. *c* 5. *c*

CHAPTER 2

Problems and Essays

1. Consumers value wine more highly. They may be willing to exchange more of other types of alcoholic beverages for a pint of wine.
2. By coming into contact with wine in France, Italy, and other European countries, American travelers have become exposed to wine, and many have found that they liked it. Possibly one could test this hypothesis by analyzing the buying habits of people before and after trips abroad to determine if there was any evidence of a change in tastes. But such a test would not be very strong.
3. First, we assume that the consumer can decide whether he prefers one market basket to another or whether he is indifferent between them.

   Second, we assume that the consumer's preferences are transitive.

   Third, we assume that the consumer always prefers more of a good to less.

   Fourth, we assume that, by adding a certain amount of one of the goods to the market basket that is not preferred, we can make it equally desirable in the eyes of the consumer.
4. The indifference curve is drawn below:

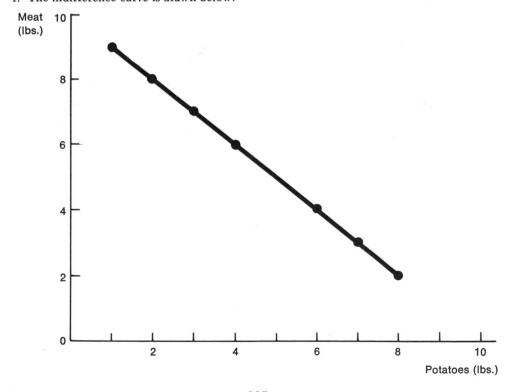

5. 1.
   It does not vary at all, at least in this range.
   No.
6. Utility is a number that indicates the level of enjoyment or preference attached to a market basket.

   In this case of ordinal utility, no particular meaning or significance attaches to the scale which is used to measure utility or to the size of the difference between the utilities attached to two market baskets. In the case of cardinal utility, it is assumed that utility is measurable in the same sense as a man's height or weight is measurable.

   Ordinal utility.
7. The consumer's budget line is drawn below:

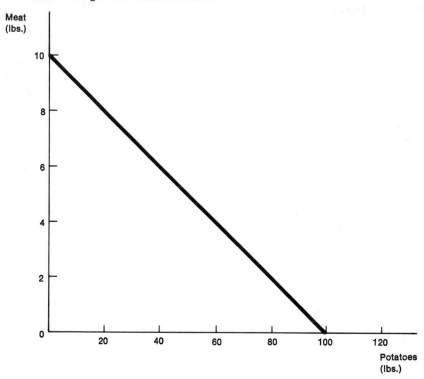

8. Under the first set of circumstances, the budget line is A. Under the second set of circumstances, it is B. And under the third set of circumstances, it is C.

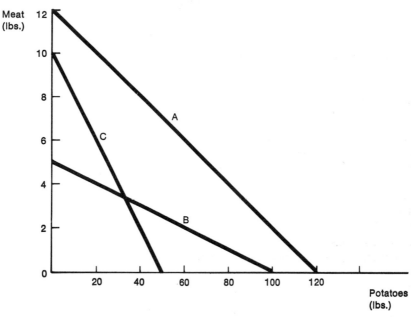

9. The theory of revealed preference deduces a consumer's preferences by looking at what he actually chooses under particular sets of circumstances.

The way in which it can be used to measure indifference curves is described in section 11 of this chapter of my text, *Microeconomics*.

No.

10. A consumer's tastes depend on his age, education, experience, and observation of others, as well as on advertising and other selling expenses, and sometimes on price.

Conspicuous consumption refers to cases where goods are consumed because they are expensive and quality is judged by price.

11. The width of the box is the total amount of good X that the two consumers together have. The height of the box is the total amount of good Y that the two consumers together have. The amount of good X that the first consumer has is measured horizontally from the origin, and the amount of good Y that he has is measured vertically from the origin. The amount of good X that the second consumer has is measured horizontally from the upper right-hand corner of the box, and the amount of good Y that he has is measured downward from the upper right-hand corner of the box.

Inserting the indifference curves of the two consumers in the box, one can find those points where one consumer's indifference curve is tangent to the other consumer's indifference curve. The locus of such points is called the contract curve. The contract curve is an optimal set of points in the sense that, if the consumers are at a point *off* the contract curve, it is always preferable for them to move to a point *on* the contract curve, since one or both can gain from the move while neither incurs a loss. The contract curve has many practical uses for this reason, one example being the allocation of fissionable materials.

12. No.

The allocation corresponding to the point where indifference curve I is tangent to indifference curve II would be better.

13. If P_b is the price of beans and P_c is the price of corn, $P_b Q_b + P_c Q_c = 50$. Since $P_b = .50$, $.5 Q_b = 50 - Q_c P_c$. Also $\partial U/\partial Q_b \div P_b = \partial U/\partial Q_c \div P_c$, which means that $\dfrac{4}{Q_b} \div .5 = \dfrac{1}{Q_c} \div P_c$. Thus, $\dfrac{8}{Q_b} = \dfrac{1}{Q_c P_c}$, or $Q_c P_c = Q_b/8$. Since $Q_b = 100 - 2 Q_c P_c$, $8 Q_c P_c = 100 - 2 Q_c P_c$, or $Q_c P_c = 10$. Thus the relationship is $Q_c = 10/P_c$.

Completion Questions

1. more; less
2. indifference
3. marginal rate of substitution
4. maximize; budget
5. tangent to
6. contract
7. negative
8. convex
9. tastes [or his income]
10. which he prefers; prefers oranges to apples; more; less
11. same
12. higher

True or False

1. False 2. True 3. False 4. False 5. True 6. False 7. False 8. True 9. False 10. False

Multiple Choice

1. *a* 2. *b* 3. *b* 4. *c* 5. *a*

CHAPTER 3

Problems and Essays

1. Yes. Because the farm price and the retail price do not vary proportionately.
2. The price elasticity of demand for a particular fuel (like oil or natural gas) is probably greater in the long run than in the short run.
3. The marginal rate of substitution is the rate at which the consumer is *willing* to substitute good X for good Y, holding his total level of satisfaction constant. Thus, if the marginal rate of substitution is three, the consumer is willing to give up three units of good Y in order to get one more unit of good X.

   The ratio of the price of good X to the price of good Y is the rate at which the consumer is *able* to substitute good X for good Y. Thus, if $P_x \div P_y$ is two, he must give up two units of good Y to get one more unit of good X.

   If the consumer is in equilibrium, the rate at which the consumer is willing to substitute good X for good Y (holding satisfaction constant) must equal the rate at which he is able to substitute good X for good Y. Otherwise it is always possible to find another market basket that will increase the consumer's satisfaction.

4. The Engel curve is as follows:

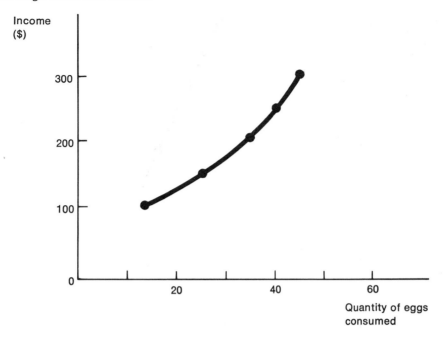

5. The shape of a consumer's Engel curve for a particular good will depend on the nature of the good, the nature of the consumer's tastes, and the level at which prices are held constant. For example, Engel curves for salt or shoelaces would generally show that the consumption of these commodities does not increase very much in response to increases in income. But goods like caviar or filet mignon might be expected to have Engel curves showing that their consumption is much more sensitive to changes in income.

6. A price-consumption curve connects the various points at which the budget line is tangent to a consumer's indifference curves, given the level of his income and the price of good Y. (Only the price of good X varies.) Reading off the amount consumed of good X at each price of good X, one can get from the price-consumption curve the basic data needed to formulate the individual demand curve.

7. The demand curve is as follows:

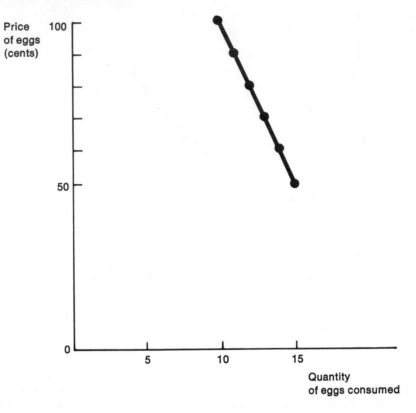

8. Three.
   Price-elastic.
   Decrease.
9. The substitution effect is the change in quantity demanded of a good resulting from a change in its price, when the level of satisfaction, or real income, is held constant.
   The income effect is the change in quantity demanded of a good due entirely to a change in real income, all prices being held constant.
   No, the substitution effect cannot be positive.
   Yes, the income effect can be positive.
10. Normal goods are goods where increases (decreases) in real income result in increases (decreases) in consumption of the good. Inferior goods are goods where the opposite is true.
    Giffen's paradox occurs when an inferior good's income effect is powerful enough to offset the substitution effect, the result being that quantity demanded is positively related to price, at least over some range of variation of price.
11. Consumer's surplus is the difference between the maximum amount that a consumer would pay and the amount that he actually pays.
    The RAND economists attempted to evaluate the loss to consumers arising from the fact that metering would lead them to consume less water by estimating the maximum amount that they would pay for this water. Because of the existence of consumer's surplus, this amount is more than what they actually paid.

12. *a.* This indifference curve is:

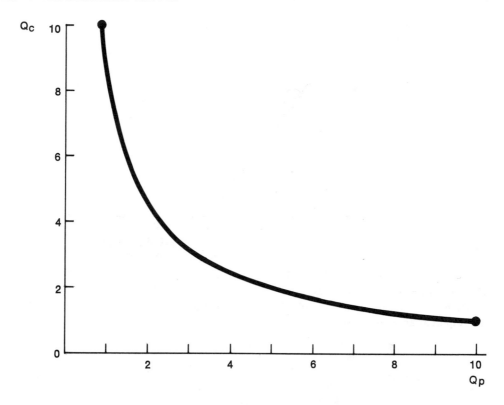

b. The budget line is $Q_c + .5\,Q_p = 100$. This line is tangent to an indifference curve when $Q_p = 100$.

c. The budget line in part *b* is tangent to an indifference curve when $Q_c = 50$ (and $Q_p = 100$).

13. Since $\partial U/\partial Q_c = Q_p$ and $\partial U/\partial Q_p = Q_c$, $Q_p \div P_c = Q_c \div P_p$. Moreover, $P_c Q_c + P_p Q_p = I$. Thus $2\,P_p Q_p = I$, and the demand curve is

$$P_p = 2\,I/Q_p.$$

14. The Laspeyres index measures the change in cost of the market basket purchased by the consumer in the *original* year. The Paasche index measures the change in cost of the market basket purchased by the consumer in the *later* year.

We can be sure that the consumer's welfare has increased if the ratio of his later money income to his earlier money income is greater than the Laspeyres price index. And we can be sure that his welfare has decreased if the ratio of his later money income to his earlier money income is less than the Paasche price index.

15. The indifference curves are as follows:

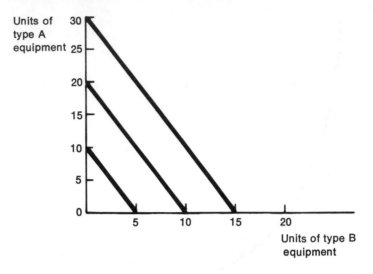

16. The budget line is the broken line.
    Given the indifference map of solid lines, the optimal point is A, where 20 units of type A equipment are purchased.

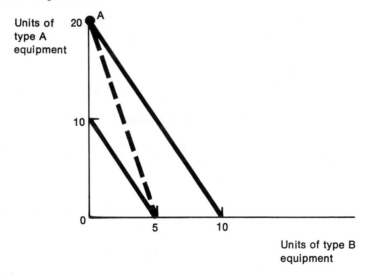

Completion Questions

1. negative
2. inflation
3. consumer's income; the amount of a good that he demands
4. elastic
5. inelastic
6. unitary elasticity
7. substitution; income

8. two
9. normal
10. $45

True or False

1. False 2. True 3. True 4. True 5. True 6. False 7. False 8. True 9. True 10. False
11. False 12. False

Multiple Choice

1. *b* 2. *c* 3. *b* 4. *a* 5. *b*

CHAPTER 4

Case for Discussion

The price elasticity of demand for Florida Indian River oranges seems to be 3.1; the price elasticity of demand for Florida Interior oranges seems to be 3.0; and the price elasticity of demand for California oranges seems to be 2.8. The cross elasticities (η_{xy}) are as follows:

| | *X* | | |
Y	Florida Indian River	Florida Interior	California
Florida Indian River	—	1.6	0.01
Florida Interior	1.2	—	0.1
California	0.2	0.1	—

Clearly, Florida Indian River and Florida Interior oranges are closer substitutes than the Florida and California oranges. This fact is of obvious use to orange growers in both parts of the country. The study is limited, of course, by the fact that it pertains to only one city at only one relatively short period of time.

Problems and Essays

1. Because there are lots of very close substitutes for a particular brand, but not for cigarettes as a whole. Yes.
2. It will result in an increase in the amount of money spent on steel.
3. A market is a group of firms and individuals that are in touch with each other in order to buy or sell some good. Basically, all markets consist primarily of buyers and sellers, although third parties like brokers and agents may be present as well.

    The market demand curve is simply the horizontal summation of the individual demand curves of all the consumers in the market.
4. If ΔP is very small, we can compute the point elasticity of demand, which is

    $$-\frac{\Delta Q}{Q} \div \frac{\Delta P}{P}.$$

    If we have data concerning only large changes in price, we can compute the arc elasticity of demand, which is $\dfrac{\Delta Q \,(P_1 + P_2)}{\Delta P \,(Q_1 + Q_2)}$.

5. $$\frac{\Delta Q\,(P_1+P_2)}{\Delta P\,(Q_1+Q_2)} = \frac{1\,(1+2)}{1\,(8+7)} = \frac{3}{15} = .20$$

$$\frac{\Delta Q\,(P_1+P_2)}{\Delta P\,(Q_1+Q_2)} = \frac{1\,(2+3)}{1\,(7+6)} = \frac{5}{13} = .38$$

$$\frac{\Delta Q\,(P_1+P_2)}{\Delta P\,(Q_1+Q_2)} = \frac{1\,(4+5)}{1\,(5+4)} = \frac{9}{9} = 1.00$$

6. The price elasticity of demand equals VD' ÷ DV. For a proof of this fact, see section 3 of this chapter of my text, *Microeconomics*.

7. First, and foremost, the price elasticity of demand for a commodity depends on the number and closeness of the substitutes that are available. If a commodity has many close substitutes, its demand is likely to be price-elastic.

   The extent to which a commodity has close substitutes depends on how narrowly it is defined. In general, one would expect that, as the definition of the market becomes narrower and more specific, the product will have more close substitutes and its demand will become more price-elastic.

   Second, it is often asserted that the price elasticity of demand for a commodity is likely to depend on the importance of the commodity in consumers' budgets. For example, the demand for thumbtacks may be quite inelastic.

   Third, it is often asserted that the price elasticity of demand for a commodity depends on the range of uses for it. If a commodity has a wide range of uses, it is often felt that its demand will be more elastic than if it can be used in only one area.

   Fourth, the price elasticity of demand for a commodity is likely to depend on the length of the period to which the demand curve pertains.

8. The income elasticity of demand is $\dfrac{\Delta Q}{Q} \div \dfrac{\Delta I}{I}$, where Q is quantity demanded and I is income.

   One would expect the income elasticity of demand generally to be higher for luxuries than for necessities.

   Engel's Law states that better-off nations spend a smaller proportion of their incomes on food than do poorer nations, the income elasticity of demand for food being quite low.

9. The cross elasticity of demand is the percentage change in the quantity of good X resulting from a 1 percent change in the price of good Y.

   The cross elasticity of demand is positive if goods X and Y are substitutes and negative if goods X and Y are complements.

10. The following table derives marginal revenue:

Quantity	Price	Total revenue	Marginal revenue
1	$10	$10	—
2	9	18	$18 − $10 = $ 8
3	8	24	24 − 18 = 6
4	7	28	28 − 24 = 4
5	6	30	30 − 28 = 2
6	5	30	30 − 30 = 0
7	4	28	28 − 30 = −2
8	3	24	24 − 28 = −4
9	2	18	18 − 24 = −6

The marginal revenue curve is as follows:

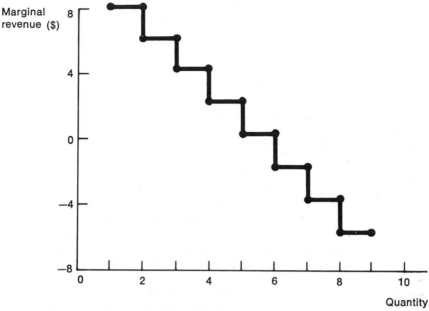

11. The marginal revenue curve is DR below.

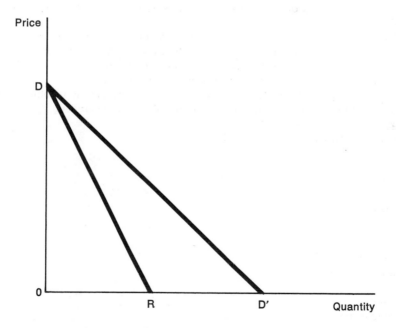

12. The firm's demand curve under perfect competition is a horizontal line.
    This is because the firm can sell all it wants without influencing the price. A very small decrease in price would result in an indefinitely large increase in the quantity it could sell, and a very small increase in its price would result in its selling nothing.

13. For students with a grasp of elementary calculus, the derivation is:

$$MR = p + q\,\frac{dp}{dq}$$

$$= p\left(1 + \frac{q}{p}\frac{dp}{dq}\right)$$

$$= p\left(1 - \frac{1}{\eta}\right)$$

For students without a knowledge of elementary calculus, a proof is given in section 11 of this chapter of my text, *Microeconomics*.

14. One method is direct market experimentation; another is to interview consumers and administer questionnaires concerning buying habits; another is to use statistical methods to extract information from past market data. Each of these methods has its problems, but the difficulties, although sometimes formidable, are not insoluble.

15. It would indicate the extent to which fare increases would decrease subway travel. For example, William Vickrey's data seem to indicate that fare increases would increase total revenue since demand is price-inelastic. Obviously this is an important fact.

16. It might indicate that both the companies and the public might be better off if steel prices were lowered somewhat, since the quantity demanded might expand more than heretofore expected.

17. Other factors—notably the general level of prices and incomes and the quality of the students—have not been held constant. Holding these factors—and the tuition rates at other universities—constant, it is almost surely untrue that large increases in tuition at this university would not cut down on the number of students demanding admission to the university.

18. There have been changes in the price of servants, the distribution of income, tastes, and other relevant factors. Taking these changes into account, there is no contradiction.

19. *a.* There would be a 3.6-percent increase in quantity demanded.
    b. There would be a 6-percent increase in quantity demanded.

20. All other things equal, you could expect that a 1-percent increase in income would result in about a 1-percent increase in the total quantity of liquor demanded.

Completion Questions

1. substitutes
2. 1-percent
3. high
4. price-elastic
5. $-\dfrac{\Delta Q}{Q} \div \dfrac{\Delta P}{P}$
6. the income elasticity of food is low
7. horizontal
8. higher
9. total revenue
10. marginal revenue
11. horizontal
12. risky

True or False

1. True 2. False 3. False 4. False 5. False 6. False 7. False 8. False 9. False 10. False 11. False 12. True

Multiple Choice

1. *a* 2. *b* 3. *a* 4. *c* 5. *b* 6. *b*

CHAPTER 5

Problems and Essays

1. It resulted in more output being obtainable from a fixed amount of capital and labor than before. Once the new machines were available, the optimal input combination was one where the capital-labor ratio was higher than before.
2. It is clear that we are unlikely to find more than about 10-20 auto firms in the United States. Since Chile produces far fewer autos, we would expect to find far fewer auto firms than this number. Engineering estimates and statistical analysis of costs are some important techniques to estimate economies of scale.
3. Yes. The marginal product of labor equals the slope of this relationship. If you plot the relationship, you will find that the slope decreases as L increases.
4. First, the making of profits generally requires time and energy, and if the owners of the firm are the managers as well, they may decide that it is preferable to sacrifice profits for leisure. Second, in an uncertain world, the concept of maximum profit is not clearly defined. Third, it is often claimed that firms pursue other objectives than profits: e.g., better social conditions, a good image, higher market share, and so forth.

   Alternative assumptions are as follows: We can assume that firms maximize utility, not profit. We can assume that they maximize some function of expected profit and the variance of profits. We can assume that they "satisfice." Or we can assume that they maximize sales subject to a profit constraint.

   Profit maximization remains the standard assumption in microeconomics because it is a close enough approximation for many important purposes, because alternative theories sometimes require unavailable data, and because it provides rules of rational behavior for firms that do want to maximize profits.
5. Technology is the sum total of society's pool of knowledge concerning the industrial arts. How much can be produced with a given set of inputs depends upon the level of technology.

   A fixed input is an input whose quantity cannot be changed during the period of time under consideration.

   A variable input is an input whose quantity can be changed during the relevant period.
6. The production function is the relationship between the quantities of various inputs used per period of time and the maximum quantity of the output that can be produced per period of time.

   The short run is that period of time in which some of the firms's inputs are fixed.

   The long run is that period of time in which all inputs are variable.

   In the short run, certain inputs are fixed in quantity, whereas this is not the case in the long run.

7. *a.* The average product curve is as follows:

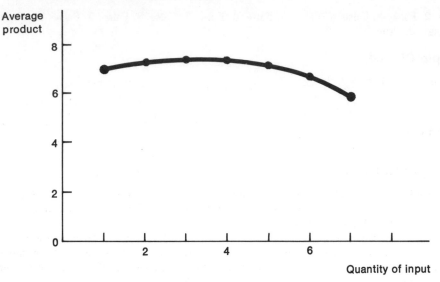

b. The marginal product curve is as follows:

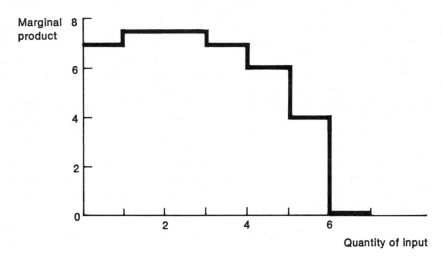

8. The law of diminishing marginal returns states that if equal increments of an input are added, the quantities of other inputs being held constant, the resulting increments in product will decrease beyond some point.

Since marginal product decreases beyond some point, the marginal product curve must turn down beyond some point.

9. The average product of OQ units of input equals the slope of OG, a straight line that connects O and G. The marginal product at OQ units of input equals the slope of VV′, the tangent at G.

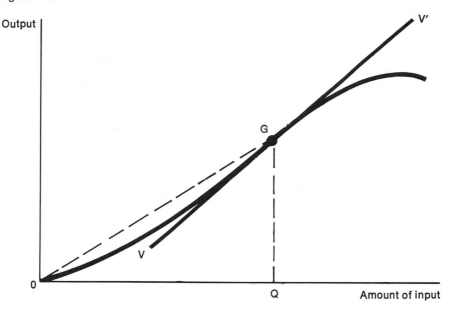

10. Stage I covers that range of utilization of variable input where the average product of the variable input is increasing.

Stage III covers that range of utilization of variable input where the marginal product of the variable input is negative.

Stage II covers that range of utilization of variable input that begins at the end of Stage I and ends at the beginning of Stage III.

The firm will not operate in Stage III, because the use of fewer units of variable input would increase the firm's output but not its costs.

The firm under these circumstances will try not to operate in Stage I because it could increase its output level by decreasing the amount of the fixed input that it uses.

11. An isoquant is a curve showing all possible (efficient) combinations of inputs that can produce a certain quantity of output.

The marginal rate of technical substitution is the rate at which one input can be substituted for another to maintain a constant output rate.

12. Letting Q be output, x_1 be the amount of labor, and x_2 be the amount of capital,

$$dQ = \frac{\partial f}{\partial x_1} dx_1 + \frac{\partial f}{\partial x_2} dx_2 \, ,$$

where f is the production function. Since $dQ = 0$, the marginal rate of technical substitution is

$$\frac{-dx_2}{dx_1} = \frac{\partial f}{\partial x_1} \div \frac{\partial f}{\partial x_2}$$

For a proof not involving calculus, see section 9 of this chapter of my text, *Microeconomics*.

-251-

13. If all inputs are increased by a certain percentage, with the result that output increases by more than this percentage, this is a case of increasing returns to scale.

   If all inputs are increased by a certain percentage, with the result that output increases by less than this percentage, this is a case of decreasing returns to scale.

   If all inputs are increased by a certain percentage, with the result that output increases by the same percentage, this is a case of constant returns to scale.

   Increasing returns to scale may be due to indivisibilities, various geometrical relations, greater specialization, probabilistic considerations, and so forth.

   Decreasing returns to scale may result from the difficulties of managing a large enterprise.

14. The three principal methods have been time-series analysis, cross-section studies, and methods based on information supplied by engineers or agricultural scientists. One problem is that the data may not pertain to efficient combinations of inputs. Another problem is the difficulty of measuring capital. Despite these and many other problems, the resulting estimates have been of considerable interest and use.

15. According to Simon, firms aim at a "satisfactory" level of profit rather than maximum profit. According to Baumol, firms maximize sales, subject to the constraint that a certain minimum profit level is attained.

16. 1.04 percent

17. It is generally larger than the coefficient of capital. See Table 5.5 of my text, *Microeconomics*.

18. Yes

19. Yes

Completion Questions

1. long run
2. "satisficing"
3. Cobb-Douglas
4. fixed in quantity
5. variable in quantity
6. variation
7. the quantity of the input
8. an extra unit of the input
9. constant
10. negative
11. negative
12. intersect

True or False

1. False 2. True 3. False 4. False 5. False 6. True 7. True 8. False 9. True 10. False
11. False 12. False

Multiple Choice

1. *c* 2. *c* 3. *a* 4. *a* 5. *a* 6. *c* 7. *b*

CHAPTER 6

Problems and Essays

1. Cost per patient day is:

$$\frac{4,700,000}{X} + .00013X,$$

which is a minimum when X is approximately equal to 190,000 patient days.

2. When $Q = 50$, $C = 16.68 + (.125)(50) + (.00439)(2500)$, which equals 33.905. When $Q = 51$, $C = 16.68 + (.125)(51) + (.00439)(2601)$, which equals 34.473. Thus, the increase in fuel cost is .568.

   This result might be of use to the managers in determining whether it would be profitable to increase output.

3. Draw the firm's isoquants, as shown below. Also draw the isocost curve corresponding to the given outlay. Clearly, point P is the input combination that maximizes output for this outlay. Since the firm's isoquant is tangent to the isocost curve at point P, the slope of the

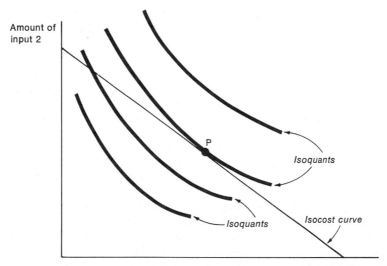

isocost curve (which equals minus one times the price of input 1 ÷ price of input 2) must equal the slope of the isoquant (which equals minus one times the marginal product of input 1 ÷ marginal product of input 2). Thus, at point P, the ratio of the marginal product to the price of each input must be the same.

4. The isocost curves are as follows:

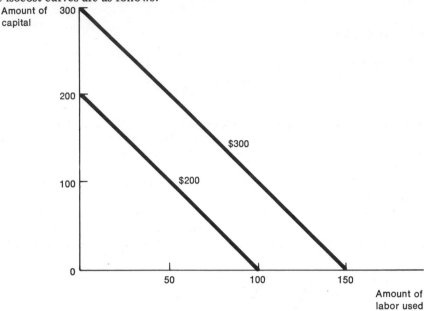

5. If the firm minimizes the cost of producing a certain output, it picks a point on the iso-quant (corresponding to this output) that is on the lowest isocost curve. This means that the optimal point is a point of tangency between this isoquant and an isocost curve. But if it is a point of tangency, the slope of the isoquant must equal the slope of the isocost curve at this point. Since the slope of the isoquant is minus one times the marginal rate of technical substitution and the slope of the isocost curve is minus one times the input price ratio, it follows that the marginal rate of technical substitution must equal the input price ratio at this point.

6. According to the opportunity or alternative cost doctrine, the cost of producing a certain product is the value of the other products that the resources used in its production could have produced instead. This doctrine lies at the heart of economic analysis and is important for proper managerial decision-making as well as for the formulation of public policy.

7. Private costs are costs to individual producers. Social costs are the total costs to society. When a firm dumps wastes into the water or the air, the private costs to the firm may be nil, but the costs to other parts of society—drinkers of the water, fishermen, people who enjoy boating, etc.—may be very great.

8. Explicit costs are the ordinary expenses that accountants include as the firm's expenses. Implicit costs are the opportunity costs of the labor and capital owned and used by the firm's owners. Unless implicit costs are considered, the firm cannot determine whether or not it is making an economic profit.

9. In the short run, some inputs, particularly the firm's plant and equipment, are fixed. In the long run, no inputs are fixed. A fixed input is one that is fixed in quantity. A variable input is one that is not fixed in quantity.

10. *a.*

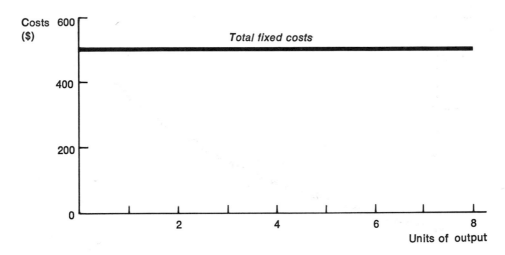

b.

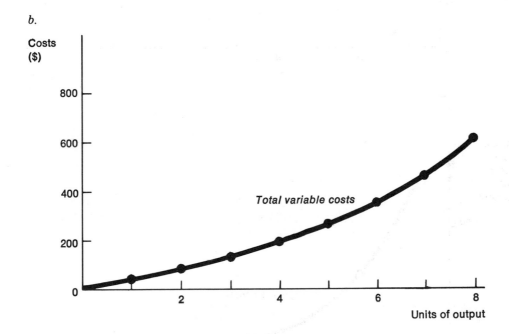

c.

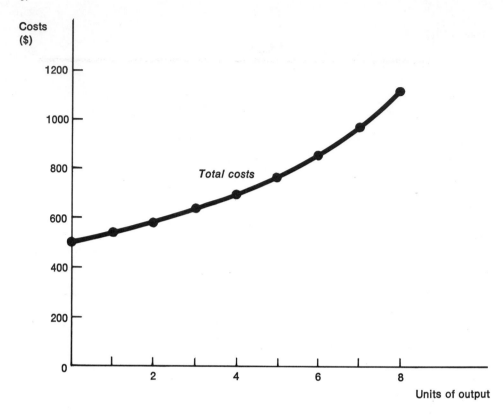

Costs
($)

Total costs

Units of output

d.

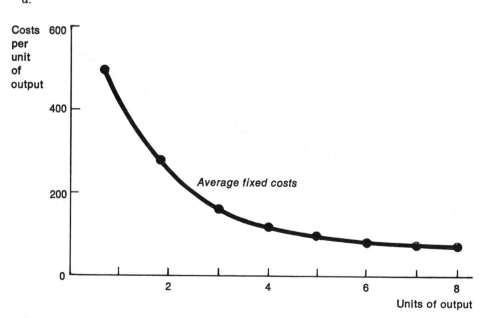

Costs
per
unit
of
output

Average fixed costs

Units of output

e.

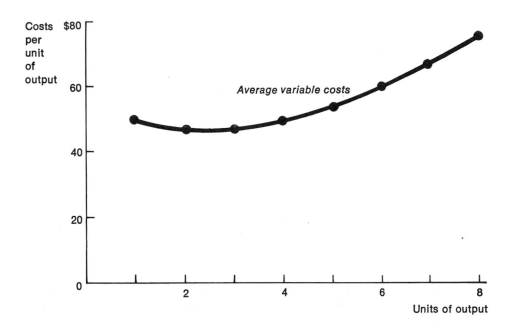

f.

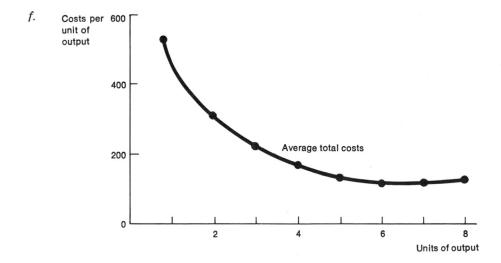

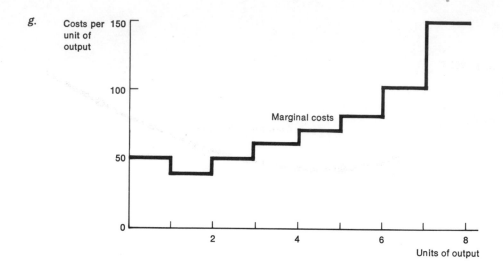

g.

11. 1000 copies sold
12. 1667 copies sold
13. *a.* The isocost curve is: Cost $= 1 \cdot L + 2 \cdot K$, or $L = \text{cost} - 2K$. The relevant isoquant is $20 = 5L \cdot K$, or $L = 4 \div K$. The point on this isoquant that is on the lowest isocost curve is $K = \sqrt{2}$ and $L = 2\sqrt{2}$.
    b. If the price of labor is $2 per unit, the optimal value of K is 2 and the optimal value of L is 2. Thus, output per unit of labor is $20 \div 2$, or 10, whereas it formerly was $20 \div 2\sqrt{2}$, or $10 \div \sqrt{2}$. Thus output per unit of labor has risen.
14. *a.* It is constant: $1.998.

    b. It declines as Q increases. Specifically, it equals $1.998 + \dfrac{2936}{Q}$.

    c. The data do not cover the range of output near and at the plant's capacity.
15. Yes
16. No

Completion Questions

1. tangent
2. fixed
3. fixed cost
4. minimum
5. long-run average cost
6. implicit costs
7. regression fallacy
8. economies and diseconomies of scale
9. law of diminishing marginal returns
10. law of diminishing marginal returns
11. average variable product
12. marginal product

True or False

1. False 2. False 3. False 4. False 5. True 6. False 7. False 8. False 9. True 10. False

Multiple Choice

1. *c* 2. *c* 3. *d* 4. *b*

CHAPTER 7

Problems and Essays

1. Profit = $5Q - 20 - 2Q - .3Q^2 = -20 + 3Q - .3Q^2$. If you plot profit against Q, you will find that it is a maximum at $Q = 5$. At $Q = 5$, profit equals $12.50 per hour.
2. If the price is $2, profit = $2Q - 20 - 2Q - .3Q^2 = -20 - .3Q^2$. If you plot profit against Q, you will find that it is a maximum at $Q = 0$. Thus, you will shut down.
3. You might use it to figure out which of a number of methods of washing cars is most profitable, given certain constraints imposed by existing capital and labor.
4. *a.* 3 or 4 units of output
   b.

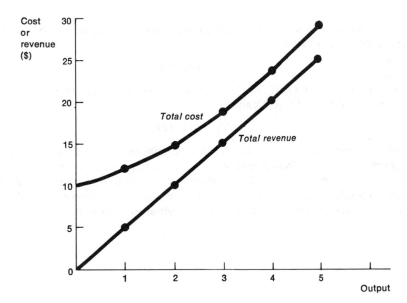

c. Price equals marginal cost between 3 and 4 units of output.

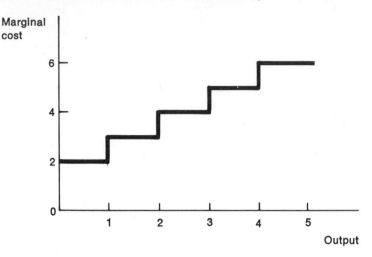

5. It will lose less money than if it shuts down completely. As long as price (P) exceeds average variable costs (AVC),

$$ATC - AFC < P$$

where ATC is average total cost and AFC is average fixed cost. The loss is $Q\,(ATC - P)$, which must be less than $Q \times AFC$, since

$$ATC - P < AFC$$

6. The product transformation curve shows the maximum amount of a particular good that can be produced, given various output levels for another good. Given a series of isorevenue lines that show the firm's revenue from various output combinations, one can find the output combination that maximizes profits. This combination is represented by the point on the product transformation curve that is on the highest isorevenue line.

7. The isorevenue line is as follows:

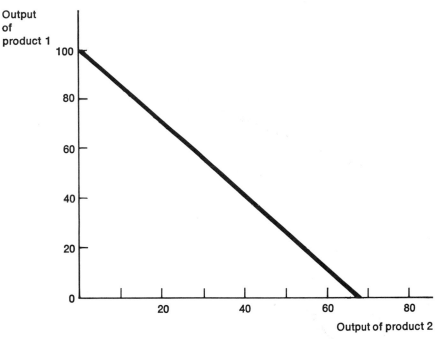

8. The firm has certain fixed amounts of a number of inputs. These limitations are constraints. The firm has available various processes. The amount of profit varies from process to process. Knowing the amount of profit to be made from a unit of output from
each process, and bearing in mind the limited amount of inputs at its disposal, the firm
must determine the activity level at which each process should be operated to maximize
profit.

   This linear programming view has at least two advantages. First, it allows the analyst to
get behind the production function. Second, it conforms more closely to the way that
businessmen view production.

9. *a.*

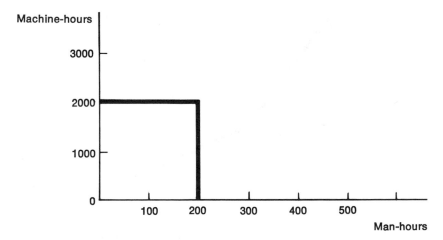

b. The ray is as follows:

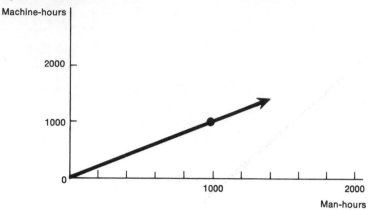

c. The rays are as follows:

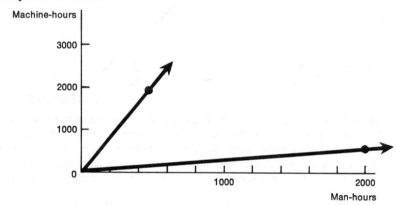

d. The isoquant is as follows:

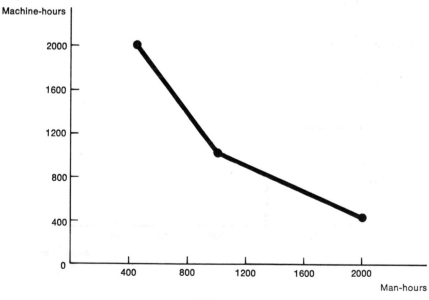

e. It should use the process that uses 1 machine-hour and 1 man-hour to produce a unit of output.

10. The solutions to the dual problem are shadow prices. For example, in the case discussed in section 14 of this chapter of my *Microeconomics*, the shadow prices show which types of capacity are bottlenecks. They show how much it would be worth to management to expand each type of capacity.

11. Linear programming has been used to determine the schedule of production rates for reservoirs to maximize profit, while meeting various technological constraints as well as commitments to supply oil.

12. See section 6 of this chapter of my text, *Microeconomics*.

13. Yes. Food cost is the objective function, and the attainment of the proper amount of calories, fats, and proteins is a series of constraints. Also, there are nonnegativity constraints.

Completion Questions

1. $5
2. 4 or 5
3. $10
4. $30
5. $10
6. $10
7. increase
8. increase
9. the marginal rate of product transformation
10. fixed

True or False

1. False 2. True 3. True 4. False 5. False 6. True 7. True 8. False 9. True 10. True

Multiple Choice

1. *b* 2. *a* 3. *c* 4. *c* 5. *b*

CHAPTER 8

Case for Discussion

The problem is that, at a price of OP_c, a shortage of natural gas will result. In other words, the quantity of new reserves supplied (OQ_s) will be less than the quantity of new reserves demanded (OQ_D). According to one estimate, new reserves were more than 50 percent short since 1961.* One obvious solution might be to discontinue regulation and to allow the price of natural gas to rise to its equilibrium level. Based on estimates of the demand and supply curves in Figure 1 (and other relevant data), Paul MacAvoy and Robert Pindyck of Massachusetts Institute of Technology conclude that deregulation (of a partial nature) would result in an elimi-

*Paul MacAvoy and Robert Pindyck, "Alternative Regulatory Policies for Dealing with the Natural Gas Shortage," *The Bell Journal of Economics and Management Science,* 1973, reprinted in part in E. Mansfield, *Microeconomics: Selected Readings,* 2d ed., New York: Norton, 1975.

nation of the shortage in the late 1970's if the field price for new gas were to increase from its 1973 level of about 30 cents per thousand cubic feet to about 60 cents in the late 1970's.* Although studies of this sort are based on a number of simplifying assumptions, they have had an impact on policy makers and researchers in this area. Recently, there has been more and more tendency for government officials to press for the loosening of regulation of natural gas prices. For example, in April 1973, President Nixon called for deregulation of wellhead prices on new contracts, and the chairman of the Federal Power Commission argued that "gas supplies are short . . . and the way to encourage more drilling and discoveries may be to let prices rise."†

Problems and Essays

1. No. In fact, Besser was found guilty of illegally monopolizing the industry in 1951 (F. M. Scherer, *Industrial Market Structure and Economic Performance*, Skokie, Ill.: Rand McNally, 1970, p. 11).

2. The arc elasticity of supply is $\dfrac{100-80}{90} \div \dfrac{6-4}{5} = 1.11$.

3. First, perfect competition requires that the product of any one seller be the same as the product of any other seller.

   Second, perfect competition requires each participant in the market, whether buyer or seller, to be so small, in relation to the entire market, that he cannot affect the product's price.

   Third, perfect competition requires that all resources be completely mobile.

   Fourth, perfect competition requires that consumers, firms, and resource owners have perfect knowledge of all relevant economic and technological data.

   No industry meets all of these characteristics, but some, like particular agricultural markets, may be reasonably close.

4. In the market period, supply is fixed, as shown below. Equilibrium price is determined by the intersection of the demand curve and the supply curve. That is, it is OP.

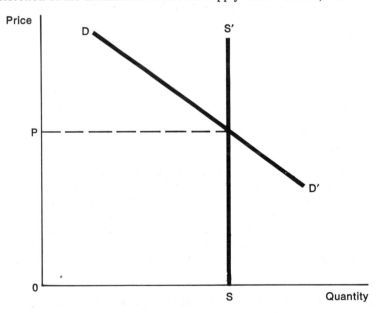

*Ibid.

†*New York Times*, April 11, 1973, p. 19.

5. $3, as shown below

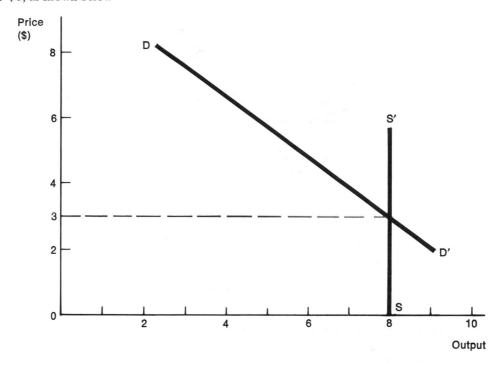

6. Given a certain price, the firm will produce an amount such that price equals marginal cost. Thus, if we vary the price, the amount that the firm will produce at each price will be given by the marginal cost curve (as long as price exceeds average variable cost).

7. If the level of the industry output does not affect the cost curves of the individual firms, the industry supply at a given price can be determined by summing up the amount supplied by each of the firms, as indicated by their marginal cost curves.

8. *a.* Equilibrium output is 600 units. Equilibrium price is $4 1/3.
   b. If price were $6, the amount demanded would be less than the amount supplied. If price were $2, the amount supplied would be less than the amount demanded.

9. If there are economic profits, new firms will tend to enter an industry. If there are economic losses, there will tend to be an outmigration of firms from the industry.

10. In the long run, firms operate where long-run marginal cost equals short-run marginal cost equals long-run average cost equals short-run average cost equals price. This means that firms operate at the minimum point of the long-run average cost curve.

11. A constant cost industry is an industry where expansion of the industry does not result in a change in input prices and firms' costs. The long-run supply curve of the industry is horizontal.

12. An increasing cost industry is an industry where expansion of the industry results in an increase in firms' costs. The long-run supply curve of the industry is upward-sloping.

13. A decreasing cost industry is an industry where expansion of the industry results in a decrease in firms' costs. The long-run supply curve of the industry is downward-sloping.

14.

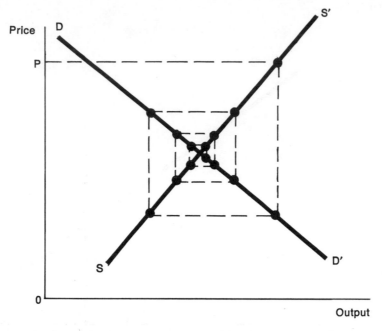

15. It is fairly close. The product is reasonably homogeneous. There is a large number of buyers and sellers. Entry is not difficult. But it does not conform to all of the assumptions of perfect competition.
16. The supply function has been shifting rapidly to the right because of rapid technological change. This has more than offset the slower movements to the right of the demand curve stemming from increases in population and income.
17. Because both the demand curve and the supply curve of agricultural commodities are quite price-inelastic.
18. No
19. It would indicate the long-run effect on quantity supplied of changes in price. Apparently, a 1 percent increase in price would result in a 4.4 percent increase in quantity supplied.
20. Yes
21. A difference of about 3.24 percent.

Completion Questions

1. supply
2. demand
3. price
4. downward-sloping
5. upward-sloping
6. horizontal
7. vertical
8. marginal cost (also average cost)
9. converge
10. less
11. cost reductions
12. common

True or False

1. True 2. False 3. False 4. False 5. False 6. False 7. False 8. False 9. True 10. True
11. True 12. True

Multiple Choice

1. *c* 2. *b* 3. *b* 4. *c* 5. *a*

CHAPTER 9

Case for Discussion

Regardless of which case (A, B, C, or D) you choose, the demand for subway travel is shown by Table 1 to be price-inelastic at the then-prevailing fare of 10 cents. This means that increases in the fare would increase total revenues. Also, it would reduce the deficit because fewer passengers would mean lower costs (or at least no higher costs). But this is not the only consideration. You would probably want to investigate how such a fare increase would affect various parts of the population—the poor, the rich, rush hour traffic, non-rush-hour traffic, and so on.

Problems and Essays

1. Because the price elasticity of demand was different in the two markets. The dental market.
2. Apparently, trucks are carrying a great deal of traffic that could be carried more cheaply by railroads. The ICC often does not allow railroads to cut their rates in order to take some of this business away from the trucks.
3. Monopoly occurs when there is one, and only one, seller in a market. The monopolist is not completely insulated from the effects of actions taken in the rest of the economy. He is affected by indirect and potential forms of competition.
4. First, a single firm may control the entire supply of a basic input that is required to make a product.

   Second, a firm may become monopolistic because the average cost of producing the product reaches a minimum at an output rate that is big enough to satisfy the entire market at a price that is profitable.

   Third, a firm may acquire a monopoly over the production of a good by having patents on the product or on certain basic processes that are used in its production.

   Fourth, a firm may become monopolistic because it is awarded a franchise by a government agency.
5. The monopolist's demand curve is the industry demand curve. Thus it is downward-sloping, whereas a perfectly competitive firm has a horizontal demand curve.

   If the monopolist is a perfect competitor in the market for inputs, the theory of cost is the same for a perfect competitor or a monopolist. Chapter 13 takes up the case where the firm is not a perfect competitor in the market for inputs.

6. *a.*

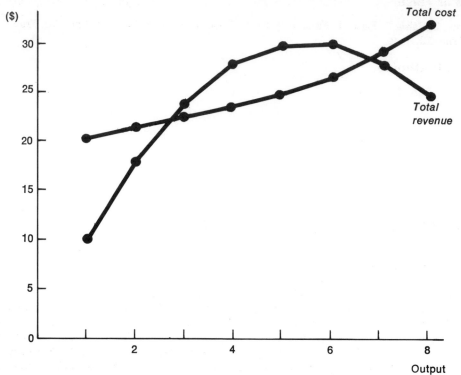

b.

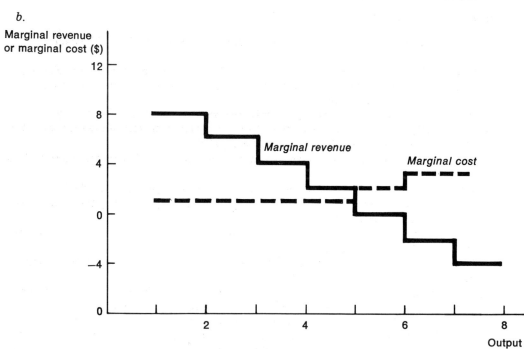

c. 5 units of output will be produced, and the price will be $6. The output is the one where marginal cost equals marginal revenue.

7. If marginal revenue exceeds marginal cost, profit can be increased by increasing output. If marginal revenue is less than marginal cost, profit can be increased by decreasing output. Profit will be a maximum when marginal revenue equals marginal cost (as long as price exceeds average variable cost).

8. He will allocate output so that the marginal costs are the same at each plant. Why? Because this is a condition for cost minimization.

9. Output is less, average costs are higher, and price is higher under monopoly than under perfect competition.

10. Basically, the idea is that the value to society of the extra output resulting from perfect competition is equal to $Q_1 C A Q_0$ whereas the cost to society of the extra output is equal to $Q_1 B A Q_0$. Thus the net loss due to the smaller output under monopoly is equal to the triangle ABC.

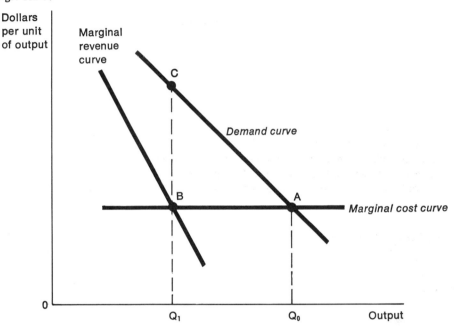

11. No. Perhaps in the labor markets where a single firm and a single union face one another.

12. Price discrimination occurs when the same commodity is sold for more than one price. For price discrimination to be feasible, it must be possible for the seller to segregate buyers into classes and that the buyers be unable to transfer the good from low-price classes to high-price classes. For price discrimination to be profitable, the price elasticity of demand must vary among classes.

13. The monopolist will set marginal revenue in the various classes equal, and the common value of marginal revenue will be set equal to marginal cost.

14. The commissions try to establish a reasonable return on a firm's existing plant. There are many difficult questions involved in determining what is "reasonable" and what is the "value" of a firm's existing plant.

15. *a.* Marginal revenue = $100 - 2Q$.
    Marginal cost = $60 + 2Q$
    Consequently, $100 - 2Q = 60 + 2Q$
    $$40 = 4Q$$
    $$10 = Q$$

    That is, you should choose an output of 10 units.

     b. Since $P = 100 - Q$, if Q equals 10, P must equal 90. So you should charge a price of 90.

16. *a.* $MR_1 = 160 - 16Q_1$

       $MR_2 = 80 - 4Q_2$

       $MC = 5 + (Q_1 + Q_2)$

       Therefore $160 - 16Q_1 = 5 + Q_1 + Q_2$

                  $80 - 4Q_2 = 5 + Q_1 + Q_2$

       Or $155 - 17Q_1 = Q_2$

              $75 - 5Q_2 = Q_1$

       Thus $155 - 17\,[75 - 5Q_2\,] = Q_2$

              $155 - 1275 + 85Q_2 = Q_2$

            $84Q_2 = 1120$

              $Q_2 = 1120/84$

     It should sell $\dfrac{1120}{84}$ units in the second market.

   b. $Q_1 = 75 - 5Q_2$

       $= 75 - 5(1120/84)$

       $= 75 - \dfrac{5600}{84}$

       $= 75 - 66\text{-}2/3$

       $= 8\text{-}1/3$

     It should sell 8-1/3 units in the first market.

17. No. At such a point marginal revenue would be negative. Thus you could increase revenue—and consequently profit—by reducing output.

20. It would have meant that monopolists would probably worry less about maximizing profits.

Completion Questions

  1. brake
  2. demand curve
  3. less
  4. unique
  5. not; profits
  6. marginal cost
  7. may or may not
  8. higher
  9. lower
10. higher
11. a single buyer
12. indeterminate

True or False

1. True 2. False 3. False 4. False 5. False 6. True 7. True 8. False 9. True 10. True

Multiple Choice

1. *e* 2. *a* 3. *a* 4. *b* 5. *a* 6. *a*

CHAPTER 10

Problems and Essays

1. One would expect relatively tightly held oligopolies to spend more on advertising than more competitive industries. Also, the line of causation may run the other way: to some extent, the high level of concentration may be due to the fact that an industry is one where advertising is an important commercial weapon.

2. Because of resale price maintenance and other techniques used by manufacturers to keep retail prices high, as well as because of the tendency for excess capacity to occur under monopolistic competition.

3. Perfect competition and pure monopoly are two polar extremes. There was a feeling that more attention should be devoted to the important "middle ground" between them. Edward Chamberlin and Joan Robinson were the principal founders of the theory of monopolistic competition. Their books appeared in 1933.

4. First, he assumes that the product is differentiated and that it is produced by a large number of firms, each firm's product being a fairly close substitute for the products of the other firms in the product group.

    Second, he assumes that the number of firms in the product group is sufficiently large so that each firm expects its actions to go unheeded by its rivals and to be unimpeded by any retaliatory measures on their part.

    Third, he assumes that both demand and cost curves are the same for all of the firms in the group.

5. One demand curve—the dd' demand curve—shows how much the firm will sell if it varies its price from the going level and if other firms maintain their existing prices. A second demand curve—the DD' demand curve—shows how much the firm will sell if it varies its price from the going level and if other firms follow suit.

6. In short-run equilibrium, the marginal revenue based on the dd' demand curve equals marginal cost at the output level where the DD' demand curve intersects the dd' demand curve.

7. The long-run equilibrium is at a point where (1) the long-run average cost curve is tangent to the dd' demand curve, and where (2) the DD' demand curve intersects the dd' demand curve and the long-run average cost curve at the tangency point.

8. For each variant of the firm's product, the firm calculates the maximum profit it can attain. Then it picks the variant of its product where the maximum profit is highest. Similarly, the firm chooses its selling expenses in an attempt to maximize profit.

9. The ideal output of a firm is the output where long-run average cost is a minimum. The ideal plant is the plant with a short-run average cost curve that is tangent to the long-run average cost curve at the ideal output.

    In long-run equilibrium under monopolistic competition, the firm will produce that quantity of output at which the dd' demand curve is tangent to the long-run average cost curve. Since the dd' demand curve slopes downward, this means that the equilibrium point must be to the left of the ideal output. In other words, there is excess capacity.

10. It is difficult to make this comparison because the product is homogeneous under perfect competition or pure monopoly but differentiated under monopolistic competition. But it seems likely that price will be higher under monopolistic competition than under perfect competition, but lower than under monopoly. Output is likely to be lower under monopolistic competition than under perfect competition, but higher than under monopoly. There is likely to be some excess capacity under monopolistic competition, but not under perfect competition.

11. Stigler attacks the concept of the group and the basic structure of Chamberlin's argument. Harrod questions the conclusions concerning excess capacity. The criticisms have a considerable amount of merit.

12. automobiles, furniture, cigarettes, tires, razor blades, and many others
13. Yes. It is quite in keeping with the excess capacity theorem.

Completion Questions

1. large number; differentiated
2. maintain
3. the same
4. more; lower
5. less; higher
6. homogeneous; differentiated
7. no effect
8. DD′ demand curve
9. dd′ demand curve
10. highly elastic

True or False

1. False 2. True 3. True 4. True 5. False 6. True 7. True 8. True 9. True 10. False

Multiple Choice

1. *a* 2. *b* 3. *c* 4. *b* 5. *c*

CHAPTER 11

Problems and Essays

1. It meant that the holders of these inventories were unlikely to sell them (and depress the price). Yes, by holding output off the market, producers could maintain prices. No.
2. The price leaders tend to be the largest firms. Also, historical factors play a role, and there is sometimes a tendency for low-cost (or medium-cost) firms to be leaders.
3. Oligopoly is a market characterized by a small number of firms and a great deal of interdependence, actual and perceived, among firms.
   Oligopoly can arise from economies of scale, or barriers to entry of various kinds.
   A pure oligopoly produces a homogeneous product, whereas a differentiated oligopoly produces a differentiated product.
4. The Cournot model assumes that each firm believes that, regardless of what output it produces, the other firm will hold its output constant at the existing level. This is not a very reasonable assumption under a wide set of circumstances.
5. The Edgeworth model assumes that each firm believes that its rivals will hold price, rather than quantity, constant. This too is not a very reasonable assumption under a wide set of circumstances.
6. The Chamberlin model assumes that firms, conscious of their interdependence, feel that the best they can do is to share the monopoly level of profit. This is more reasonable because it recognizes that firms learn and recognize their interdependence.
7. The kinked oligopoly demand curve is more elastic for price increases than for price decreases. It does not explain the level of price, but it does help to explain the rigidity of price.
8. The basic elements are the players, the rules of the game, the payoffs of the game, and the information conditions that exist during the game.

Two-person zero-sum games are not very realistic descriptions of actual market conditions.

9. Firm I will choose strategy A.
   Firm II will choose strategy 2.
10. Two-person zero-sum games are not very realistic descriptions of market conditions, and the theory of more complicated and realistic games is not well developed. These criticisms are important. Nonetheless, game theory is a suggestive framework for analysis.
11. When a collusive arrangement is made openly and formally, it is called a cartel.
    A perfect cartel will determine the marginal cost curve for the cartel as a whole. Then it will produce the output where marginal cost equals marginal revenue, and it will charge the price at which it can sell that output.
    No.
12. Because members have a great incentive to "cheat." This tendency existed among the electrical equipment manufacturers. One collusive agreement after another was drawn up in the 1950's, but after a while some firms began in each case to pursue an independent price policy.
13. The dominant-firm model assumes that the dominant firm sets the price for the industry, but that it lets the other firms sell all they want at that price.
    On the other hand, the barometric-firm model assumes that there is one firm that is usually the first to make changes in price that are generally accepted by other firms in the industry. The barometric firm may not be the largest or most powerful, but it is a reasonably accurate interpreter of changes in basic cost and demand conditions in the industry as a whole.
14. According to cost-plus pricing, firms estimate the cost per unit of output (at some assumed output level) and add a certain percentage markup to obtain the price.
    No.
15. Smallness of the market relative to optimum size of firm, large capital requirements, unavailability of natural resources, patents, and franchises.
16. Price and profits are likely to be higher than under perfect competition, but lower than under monopoly. Output is likely to be more than under monopoly, but less than under perfect competition (if the demand curve is the same).
17. *a.* Since $Q = 300 - P$, and the demand for the firm's output is $Q - Q_r$, it follows that the firm's demand curve is:

$$Q_b = Q - Q_r = (300 - P) - 49P$$
$$= 300 - 50P,$$
or
$$P = 6 - .02\,Q_b$$

Thus, the firm's marginal revenue curve is $MR = 6 - .04\,Q_b$. And since its marginal cost curve is $2.96\,Q_b$, it follows that

$$6 - .04\,Q_b = 2.96\,Q_b$$
$$Q_b = 2$$

b. Since $P = 6 - .02\,Q_b$, and $Q_b = 2$, it follows that

$$P = 6 - .02\,(2) = 5.96$$

That is, the price should be 5.96.

c. Since $Q = 300 - P$, and $P = 5.96$, it follows that

$$Q = 300 - 5.96 = 294.04.$$

That is, the industry output is 294.04.

18. There really is no way that we can answer this question with any certainty.
19. Yes. Many products are dominated by only a few sellers, and there are substantial barriers to entry.
21. Yes
22. Oligopoly is very likely in tractor manufacturing, but not (for this reason at least) in fresh-meat packing.
23. Yes. Because of possible entry, for one thing.
25. Yes. One would expect that the profit rate would be higher in more concentrated industries.

Completion Questions

1. changes
2. steel (among many others)
3. pure
4. its existing level
5. constant
6. monopoly
7. maintain their present price
8. lower their price too
9. definite optimal pure strategy
10. always exist

True or False

1. False 2. True 3. False 4. True 5. False 6. True 7. True 8. False 9. False 10. True

Multiple Choice

1. b 2. a 3. a 4. b 5. c

CHAPTER   12

Problems and Essays

1. Your profit equals $5Q - 4.5L$. Substituting for Q, your profit equals

$$5[-0.8 + 4.5L - .3L^2] - 4.5L = -4 + 18L - 1.5L^2 .$$

If you plot profit against L, you will find that it is a maximum at $L = 6$. Thus, you should employ 6 men. $50.
2. 7 men. 5 men.

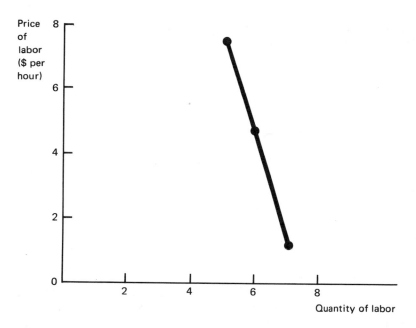

3. A person's income depends largely on the quantity of inputs he owns and the prices of these inputs. Input prices play a very important role.

4. It follows from the fact that the marginal rate of technical substitution must equal the input price ratio that

$$\frac{P_x}{MP_x} = \frac{P_y}{MP_y} = \ldots = \frac{P_z}{MP_z}$$

Also, the extra cost of producing an extra unit of product, if the extra production comes about by increasing the use of any input, must equal the ratio of the price of the input to its marginal product. Consequently, each of the ratios shown above equals marginal cost.

5. This follows from problem 2. Since MC = Price under perfect competition, it follows that

$$\frac{P_x}{MP_x} = \frac{P_y}{MP_y} = \ldots = \frac{P_z}{MP_z} = \text{Price.}$$

Thus, MP_x times Price = P_x; MP_y times Price = P_y; and so forth.

6. The demand curve for labor is:

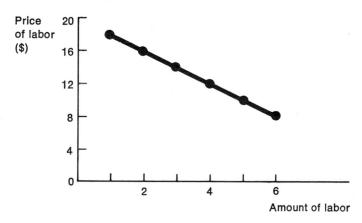

7. First, the more easily other inputs can be substituted for a certain input, the more price-elastic is the demand for this input.

   Second, the larger the price elasticity of demand for the product that the input helps to produce, the larger the price elasticity of demand for the input.

   Third, the greater the price elasticity of supply of the other inputs, the greater is the price elasticity of demand for this input.

   Fourth, the price elasticity of demand for an input is likely to be greater in the long run than in the short run.

8. A backward-bending supply curve can occur when the person supplying the input can use it himself. As the price of the input increases, the person supplying the input becomes richer. If the income effect more than offsets the substitution effect, the result will be that the person supplies less of the input.

9. OP_0 is not an equilibrium price because at this price the quantity supplied exceeds the quantity demanded. Since this is the case, inventories would build up and sellers would begin to reduce the price.

   OP_1 is not an equilibrium price because at this price the quantity demanded exceeds the quantity supplied. Since this is the case, inventories would fall and shortages might develop, with the result that the price would be bid up.

10. This is because a rent is, by definition, a payment to an input that is in fixed supply. It is important because, if the government imposes a tax on rents, there will be no effect on the supply of resources to the economy.

11. A quasi-rent is a payment to any input that is in temporarily fixed supply.

12. If a firm maximizes profit, it hires each type of plumber in such amounts that:

$$MP_s \cdot MR = P_s$$
$$MP_u \cdot MR = P_u$$

where MP_s is the marginal product of skilled plumbers, MP_u is the marginal product of unskilled plumbers, MR is marginal revenue, P_s is the wage of skilled plumbers, and P_u is the wage of unskilled plumbers. Thus, $P_s \div P_u = MP_s \div MP_u$.

13. Differences in costs of training, occupational expenses, stability of employment, geographical differences in the cost of living, and so forth.

14. The elasticity of substitution measures the extent to which the capital-labor ratio changes in response to changes in the ratio of the price of capital to the price of labor. Whether or not an increase in the price of labor relative to the price of capital will decrease the ratio of capital income to labor income depends on the elasticity of substitution.

15. The wage, P_L, will equal the price of the product, P, times the marginal product of labor, which equals

$$\frac{\partial Q}{\partial L} = .8 L^{-.2} K^{.2} = \frac{.8Q}{L}.$$

Thus $P_L = \frac{.8Q}{L} \cdot P$, which means that

$$\frac{P_L L}{PQ} = .8 .$$

Since $P_L \cdot L$ equals the total wages paid by the firm and PQ equals its revenues, this completes the proof.

16. The demand curve for scientists and engineers moved to the left. The wage rate tended to be sticky, with the result that many scientists and engineers were out of work, at least temporarily.

17. They postulated a stickiness on the part of the wage for scientists and engineers, this stickiness resulting in apparent shortages. They concluded that the apparent shortage would be over when the necessary wage increases occurred.

18. On the basis of cross-section data, Stuart Altman and Alan Fechter estimated the supply curve for manpower to the defense establishment. Then on the basis of independent estimates of the necessary size of the armed forces, they estimated the wage required to obtain this much labor. The total cost to the Department of Defense was this wage times the number of people in the armed forces.

19. It is backward-bending. See answer to question 6 above.

Completion Questions

1. reduce
2. the price of the product
3. the price of the product
4. rent
5. the ratio of the price of capital to the price of labor
6. decrease
7. fixed; supply
8. long; short
9. smaller
10. differences in training costs, occupational expenses, cost of living, stability of employment, and so forth.

True or False

1. False 2. True 3. False 4. True 5. False 6. False 7. True 8. False 9. True 10. False

Multiple Choice

1. *c* 2. *c* 3. *c* 4. *b* 5. *b*

CHAPTER 13

Problems and Essays

1. It can be incorporated by asserting that the current wage is a floor that almost never will be penetrated in the course of collective bargaining. It implies that an assumption of downward wage flexibility is unrealistic.

2. The Auto Workers and Steelworkers asked for a "guaranteed" annual wage in the 1940's. Also, pensions, health, and welfare funds are other examples.

3. The firm will set the marginal revenue product of each input equal to the input's price. Since the former measures the extra revenue derived from an extra unit of input and the latter measures the extra cost of an extra unit of input, profit cannot be a maximum if the latter is less than the former—or more than the former. It can only be a maximum when they are equal.

4. *a.* four units of labor. For reason, see below:

Amount of labor	Total product	Marginal product	Price of good	Total revenue	Marginal revenue product
2	23	10	5.00	$115	n.a.
3	32	9	4.00	128	$13
4	40	8	3.50	140	12
5	47	7	3.00	141	1
6	53	6	2.00	106	−35

b. 3 units of labor
c. 4 units of labor
d. 5 units of labor
e. The demand curve is:

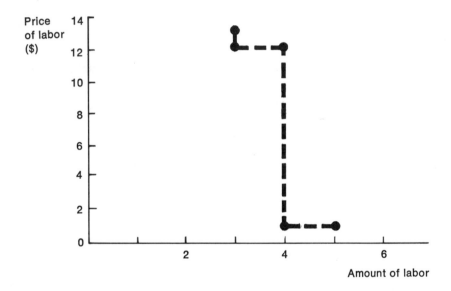

5. By definition, the marginal revenue product is $\Delta R \div \Delta I$, where ΔR is the change in total revenue and ΔI is the change in the quantity of the input. Since marginal revenue (MR) equals $\Delta R \div \Delta Q$, where ΔQ is the change in output, it follows that the marginal revenue product equals $MR \; \Delta Q \div \Delta I$. And since marginal product (MP) equals $\Delta Q \div \Delta I$, it follows that the marginal revenue product equals $MR \cdot MP$.
6. Monopsony is a case where there is a single buyer. Company towns or mill towns are sometimes examples of monopsony.
7. Perfectly competitive, because the wage will be higher.
8. Monopsonistic, because the wage will be lower.
9. A profit-maximizing monopsonist will hire an input up to the point where its marginal product times the firm's marginal revenue equals the marginal expenditure for the input.
10. They can shift the supply curve for labor to the left, try to get the employer to pay a higher wage while allowing some of the supply of labor forthcoming at this higher wage to find no opportunity for work, or try to shift the demand for labor upward and to the right.

11. The union might want to maximize the wage, subject to the constraint that a certain number of its members be employed. Or it might want to maximize the wage bill. It is difficult to summarize union goals adequately and simply.
12. Far too little is known about their effects. Empirical studies have generally been based on comparisons of wage increases in unionized industries with those in nonunion industries. Such evidence is difficult to interpret, and the findings have not been clear-cut.
13. They seem to indicate that the strength of the union was directly related to the relative height of wages in the industry.
15. Because union contracts tend to introduce rigidity in wage structures.
16. Wages of baseball stars may be lower than in a competitive market.
17. Although unions may have raised wages in some industries, they may not have done so in others. Moreover, this finding depends on things other than the wage rate.

Completion Questions

1. the input's marginal revenue product
2. $MRP = MR \cdot MP$, whereas $VMP = P \cdot MP$
3. value-of-marginal-product schedule
4. horizontal summation
5. a single buyer
6. a company town where a single firm is the sole buyer of labor.
7. above
8. the input's marginal revenue product
9. less
10. lower

True or False

1. True 2. True 3. True 4. True 5. False 6. False 7. False 8. False 9. True 10. True

Multiple Choice

1. *c* 2. *b* 3. *b* 4. *a* 5. *b* 6. *c*

CHAPTER   14

Case for Discussion

The problem was attacked as follows: The first step was to construct an Edgeworth box diagram. Figure 1 shows what the resulting box diagram looked like. Any point in the diagram represented a possible allocation of the two goods, airplanes and fissionable material, between the two "consumers," the strategic mission and the tactical mission. For example, point P represents a case where the strategic mission gets OU units of aircraft and OV units of fissionable material, and the tactical mission gets (OA – OU) units of aircraft and (OM – OV) units of fissionable material.

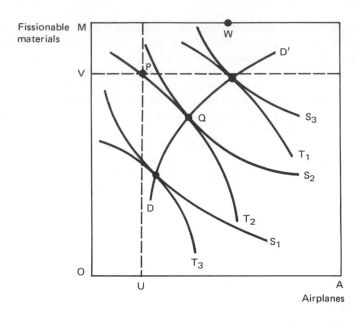

The two "consumers" are not ordinary consumers. They are military missions. What do indifference curves mean in such a situation? Consider the tactical mission's indifference curve, T_1. Each point on T_1 represents a combination of aircraft and fissionable material that results in the same number of tactical targets expected to be destroyed. The fictitious consumer, "the tactical mission," is viewed as being interested in maximizing the expected number of tactical targets that can be destroyed. In other words, the expected number of tactical targets that can be destroyed is a measure of this consumer's "utility." Thus he is indifferent among all of the points on T_1. And he clearly prefers indifference curve T_2 to indifference curve T_1. Similarly, consider the strategic mission's indifference curve, S_1. Each point on S_1 represents a combination of aircraft and fissionable material that results in the same number of strategic targets expected to be destroyed. The fictitious consumer, "the strategic mission," is viewed as being interested in maximizing the expected number of strategic targets that can be destroyed. In other words, the expected number of strategic targets that can be destroyed is a measure of the consumer's utility. Thus he is indifferent among all of the points on S_1, and he prefers S_2 to S_1.

We know that any allocation of aircraft and fissionable materials that is represented by a point that is not a point of tangency between an indifference curve of the tactical mission and an indifference curve of the strategic mission is not an optimal allocation. For example, point P is not an optimal allocation, since it is not a point of tangency between an indifference curve of the tactical mission and an indifference curve of the strategic mission. Why isn't P an optimal allocation? Because if we hold constant the expected number of tactical targets that can be destroyed (the "utility" of the tactical mission), we can increase the expected number of strategic targets that can be destroyed (the "utility" of the strategic mission) by moving to point Q. The locus of optimal points—the contract curve—is shown by DD'.

Having constructed the contract curve, what did the economists conclude? Recall that the existing allocation assigned all of the nation's stockpile of fissionable material to the strategic mission and none to the tactical mission. Thus, the existing allocation was at point W. According to the economist's calculations, this point was not on the contract curve, DD'. Consequently, the existing allocation was shown to be suboptimal, a movement to the contract curve being called for. Specifically, the stockpile of fissionable material needed to be reallocated, some atomic weapons being reserved for the tactical mission. However, this analysis could not indicate which particular point on the contract curve should be chosen, since this decision hinged on whether we wanted to increase our strategic capability at the expense of our tactical capability, or vice versa. On the basis of the information given here, no judgment on this score could be made.*

Problems and Essays

1. In input-output analysis, it is recognized that industries often use each others' products. Yes.
2. Unless one is willing to specify something about their shape, many important questions simply cannot be answered.
3. An analysis that takes account of the interrelationships among prices in various markets is called a general equilibrium analysis. This in contrast to partial equilibrium analysis, which assumes that changes in price can occur in whatever market is being studied without causing significant changes in price in other markets, which in turn affect the market being studied.
4. Partial equilibrium analysis is adequate in cases where the effect of a change in market conditions in one market has little repercussion on prices in other markets. However, if the effects of a change in market conditions in one market result in important repercussions on other prices, a general equilibrium analysis may be required.
5. A state of general equilibrium is achieved when consumers are maximizing utility (subject to budget constraints), resource owners are providing as much of various inputs as they choose, firms are maximizing profit (subject to technological constraints), and all markets are cleared. Modern work has established that in a perfectly competitive economy a state of general equilibrium can be achieved under a fairly wide set of conditions.
6. Arrow and Debreu assume that there are not increasing returns to scale, at least one primary input must be used to produce each good, each consumer can supply all primary inputs, the amount supplied by a consumer must not exceed his initial stock, each consumer's utility function is continuous, his wants cannot be satiated, and his indifference curves are convex. These conditions are sufficient but not necessary.
8. Recognizing the interdependence among various parts of the economy, input-output analysis attempts to determine the amount that each industry must produce in order to fulfill certain targets for the economy as a whole. It assumes that production coefficients are fixed.
9. a. $E = .1E + .3X +$ final consumption of electric power, where E is output of electric power and X is output of coal.
   b. $X = .5E + .1X +$ final consumption of coal.
   c. $C = .2E + .9C +$ final consumption of chemicals, where C is output of chemicals.
   d. $X = .5E + .1X + 50$
   $E = .1E + .3X + 100$
   $C = .2E + .9C + 50$
   Solution: $C = 818, E = 159, X = 144$.
   Thus, $159 million of electric power must be produced.
   e. $144 million of coal

*For further discussion of this problem, see S. Enke, "Using Costs to Select Weapons," *American Economic Review*, May 1965, and "Some Economic Aspects of Fissionable Materials," *Quarterly Journal of Economics*, May 1964. This example is taken largely from these papers.

f. $818 million of chemical

g. $.2E + .6X + .1C = 200$. Thus, $200 million of labor.

10. Changes in input prices and changes in technology.

11. Find those points where one consumer's indifference curve is tangent to the other consumer's indifference curve. The contract curve is an optimal set of points in the sense that, if the consumers are at a point off the contract curve, it is always preferable for them to move to a point on the contract curve, since one or both can gain from the move while neither incurs a loss.

12. Each point on the contract curve in such a box diagram corresponds to a certain level of production of each good. Plot these pairs of production levels, one against the other. The result is the product transformation curve.

13. Construct an Edgeworth box diagram where the upper right-hand corner of the box is the point on the product transformation curve corresponding to the amount of each commodity to be produced. Then find the point on the contract curve where the consumers' indifference curves have a common slope equal to that of the product transformation curve at the point corresponding to the amount of each commodity produced. This point on the contract curve indicates the optimal distribution of commodities between the consumers. The optimal allocation of inputs is indicated by the point on the production contract curve corresponding to the specified point on the product transformation curve.

16. No.

Completion Questions

1. little
2. general equilibrium analysis
3. general equilibrium; perfectly competitive
4. input-output analysis
5. interdependence
6. input-output analysis; fixed
7. product transformation curve
8. contract curve
9. marginal rate of substitution between the goods
10. move to a point on the contract curve.

True or False

1. False 2. False 3. False 4. True 5. False 6. False 7. False 8. True 9. True 10. False

Multiple Choice

1. *a* 2. *a* 3. *c* 4. *d* 5. *a* 6. *a*

CHAPTER 15

Problems and Essays

1. When one band is playing, there may be external economies accruing to customers of other cafes. But when lots of them play, there may be external diseconomies because it is impossible to hear any of them properly.

2. By not taking account of the effects on other parts of the firm, policies which produce optimal results—looking at the division alone—may yield results that are far from optimal for the whole firm.

3. There is no scientifically meaningful way to compare the utility levels of different individuals. Consequently, we cannot tell whether one distribution of income is better than another.

4. First, the marginal rate of substitution between two commodities must be the same for any two consumers consuming both commodities.

   Second, the marginal rate of technical substitution between two inputs must be the same for any pair of producers using both inputs.

   Third, the marginal rate of substitution between any two commodities must be the same as the marginal rate of transformation between these two commodities for any producer.

   These conditions are necessary but not sufficient for optimality.

5. No. I should trade you some peanut butter in exchange for some jelly.

6. For example, suppose that, for the first producer, the marginal product of labor is twice that of capital, whereas for the second producer the marginal product of labor is three times that of capital. Then, if the first producer gives one unit of labor to the second producer in exchange for 2.5 units of capital, both firms can expand their output.

7. Suppose for simplicity that there is only one consumer. The optimal point on the product transformation curve is the point on the consumer's highest indifference curve. This is a point where the product transformation curve is tangent to an indifference curve. Thus, the slope of the product transformation curve—the marginal rate of transformation (times minus one)—must equal the slope of the indifference curve—the marginal rate of substitution (times minus one).

8. If marginal cost varies, it is possible to reduce the total cost of the existing output by transferring production from firms with high marginal cost to firms with low marginal cost. Quota schemes related to agricultural price supports can result in differences among firms in marginal cost.

9. For each point on the product transformation curve, find the optimal allocation of output between the two consumers. Then plot the utility of one consumer against the utility of the other consumer.

10. A social welfare function shows society's evaluation of various states of the world. Given a social welfare function, one can obtain social indifference curves to couple with the utility-possibility curve. The optimal distribution of income is at the point on the utility-possibility curve that is on the highest social indifference curve.

11. Yes. No.

13. Because of price changes.

14. An external economy occurs when an action taken by an economic unit results in uncompensated benefits to others. An external diseconomy occurs when an action taken by an economic unit results in uncompensated costs to others. Too little is produced of goods generating external economies; too much is produced of goods generating external diseconomies.

15. Basic research results in important external economies. Consequently, there seems to be a good case for the government (or some other agency not motivated by profit) to support basic research. Too little would be supported by a perfectly competitive economy.

16. A public good is a good that one person can enjoy without reducing the enjoyment it gives others. Also, the consumer frequently cannot be made to pay for a public good, because he cannot be barred from using it (whether or not he pays) or because it is obligatory for everyone to use it.

No.

17. Arrow showed that, under conditions that seem to be a sensible basis for democratic community decision-making, it is impossible to make a choice among all sets of alternatives without violating some of the conditions. His work has led to a much clearer understanding of the relationships between individual preferences and social choice.

18. The theory of the second best shows that piecemeal attempts to force fulfillment of the optimality conditions can easily be a mistake. So long as some conditions remain unfulfilled, there is no assurance that a reduction of the number of unfulfilled conditions will result in increased welfare.

19. If average costs decline with output, marginal cost is below average cost, the result being that marginal-cost pricing will result in a deficit. Public subsidy is one possible answer under these circumstances.

20. Government requirement of minimum schooling, probably accomplished through government subsidy.

22. Yes.

23. It prevents water rights from being transferred from less valuable to more valuable uses, thus interfering with the optimal allocation of water.

24. It means that water will be used more extensively in low-price uses—and less extensively in high-price uses—than would be the case if water were allocated efficiently.

Completion Questions

1. no scale
2. value judgment
3. contract curve
4. contract curve
5. product transformation curve
6. the same prices
7. the same prices
8. external diseconomy of production
9. external economy of production
10. public

True or False

1. True 2. False 3. True 4. True 5. False 6. False 7. False 8. True 9. False 10. False

Multiple Choice

1. *c* 2. *b* 3. *c* 4. *d* 5. *a* 6. *b*

CHAPTER 16

Problems and Essays

1. The patent holders have added to the patent exchange agreements provisions specifying prices, market shares, and so forth. Electric lights, glass bottles, eyeglasses, magnesium, synthetic rubber, titanium paint pigments, among many others.

2. To the extent that the sizable financial and R and D resources of the oil companies are brought to bear on coal technology, it may result in a more rapid rate of technological change. However, if the oil firms feel that it is not in their interests to advance coal technology, there may be little or no such effect.

3. Technological change is the advance of knowledge concerning the industrial arts, such advance often taking the form of new processes and products.

    Certain types of technological change can be measured by the shift in the production function.

    Not with new final products.

4. Technological change is an advance in knowledge, whereas a change in technique is a change in the utilized method of production.

    Yes.

    Yes.

5. If technological change results in a greater percentage reduction in capital input than in labor input, it is capital-saving; if it results in a greater percentage reduction in labor input than in capital input, it is labor-saving; if it results in equal percentage reductions in labor input and capital input, it is neutral.

    For a description of how the isoquants shift in each case, see section 4 of this chapter of my text, *Microeconomics*.

6. Capital-embodied changes in technology must be embodied in new equipment if they are to be utilized. Disembodied technological change consists of better methods and organization that improve the efficiency of both old capital and new.

    Examples of capital-embodied technological change are the diesel locomotive and catalytic cracking. Examples of disembodied technological change are various advances in industrial engineering.

7. No.

    It is influenced by many factors other than the rate of technological change—for example, changes in capital per worker.

    Yes.

8. The total productivity index is the relative increase in output divided by a weighted average of the relative increase in labor input and the relative increase in capital input.

    It takes explicit account of capital input as well as labor input.

    If the production function is $Q = \alpha(t)[bL + cK]$.

9. Since they equate the effects of technological change with whatever increase in output is unexplained by other inputs, they may not isolate the effects of technological change alone. They contain the effects of whatever inputs may have been excluded or misspecified.

10. The amount of resources devoted to improving an industry's technology, which in turn depends on the rewards from particular kinds of technological change and on factors that determine their costs. Also, the quantity of resources devoted to improving the capital goods and other inputs it uses. Also, the industry's market structure and its relation to government objectives such as defense.

11. Research is aimed at the creation of new knowledge. Development is aimed at the reduction of research findings to practice. R and D is aimed at the reduction of uncertainty; it is a learning process.

12. When the cost of running each effort is small and when the prospective amount of learning is great.
13. The size and complexity of the product being developed, the extent of the advance in performance that is sought, the available stock of knowledge, components, and materials, the development time, and the development strategy used.
14. An innovation is the first application of an invention. There is commonly a lag of ten years or more. An invention has little or no economic significance until it is applied.
15. The profitability of the innovation and the size of investment required to use the innovation. Also, the industry's market structure, the policies of labor, and the rate at which the supply of the innovation can be increased may be important.
16. They argue that firms under perfect competition have fewer resources to devote to research and experimentation than do firms under imperfect competition. Moreover, they argue that unless a firm has sufficient control over the market to reap the rewards of an innovation, the introduction of the innovation may not be worthwhile.

   Defenders of perfect competition retort that there is likely to be less pressure for firms to innovate in imperfect markets. Also, they say that there are advantages in having a large number of independent decision-making units, there being less chance that an important technological advance will be blocked by the faulty judgment of a few men.
17. No. There is no evidence that giant firms are needed in most industries to insure rapid technological advance and rapid utilization of new techniques.
18. The price of the relevant information should be set equal to marginal cost, which is often practically zero. (Only static efficiency is considered here.)
19. No. Many factors other than technological change also influence output per man-hour.
20. Differences in R and D expenditures and economies of scale, among others.
21. A profit-maximizing firm generally will not scrap existing equipment merely because somewhat better equipment is available. The new equipment must be sufficiently better to offset the fact that the old equipment is already paid for, whereas this is not the case for the new.
22. Uncertainty concerning the technical and economic feasibility of the process, difficulty in interesting oil firms in the process, the lag involved in disseminating information concerning the existence and characteristics of the process, and so forth.
23. Technological change shifts the production function, thus offsetting the tendency toward diminishing returns.
24. No.

Completion Questions

1. society's pool of knowledge
2. change
3. constant returns to scale
4. capital-saving
5. labor-saving
6. the relative increase in output divided by a weighted average of the relative increase in labor input and the relative increase in capital input
7. uncertainty
8. increases
9. innovation
10. 10

True or False

1. False 2. False 3. False 4. True 5. True 6. True 7. False 8. False 9. True 10. False

Multiple Choice

1. *c* 2. *b* 3. *b* 4. *b* 5. *c* 6. *b*

CHAPTER 17

Problems and Essays

1. The exclusion principle operates when whether or not a person consumes a good is contingent on whether or not he or she pays the price. Yes. Frequently not.
2. Rivalry in consumption holds for goods where, if one person consumes them, someone else cannot consume them too. Yes. No.
3. Because a person is likely to feel that the total output of the good will not be affected significantly by his action. He or she will be likely to make no contribution to supporting the good, although he or she will use whatever output of the good is forthcoming.
4. Horizontally. See Chapter 4.
5. Vertically. See section 3 of this chapter of my text, *Microeconomics*.
6. Build the road from X to Y, because it will maximize the benefits to be derived from the fixed budget of $10 million.
7. Build the roads from X to Y and from X to Z, because these projects have benefit-cost ratios exceeding one.
8. In broad problems of choice, it frequently is more difficult to quantify benefits and make them comparable. Yes.
9. You might try to estimate how much people could make if they could use the time saved in various alternative pursuits, but this is difficult to estimate. See the article by Prest and Turvey in Mansfield, *Microeconomics: Selected Readings*, 2d ed., New York: Norton, 1975.
10. The Corps of Engineers included many kinds of benefits that the railroad consultants did not include, such as enhancement of waterfront land values. Also, the Crops of Engineers made a lower estimate of the costs. To some extent, as Prest and Turvey point out, the difference may be "due to the facts that the Corps likes to build canals and that the consultants were retained by the railroads."
12. External diseconomies from waste disposal.
13. An effluent fee is a fee that a polluter must pay to the government for discharging waste. It brings the private cost of waste disposal closer to the social cost. Yes, for example, in the Ruhr Valley.
14. The fact that the public is concerned is not a proof that the extra benefits exceed the extra costs. Unfortunately, however, it is extremely difficult to answer this question in any definitive sense.
15. A better criterion would be one that is based on a comparison of costs and benefits, assuming that these costs and benefits can be measured, at least roughly.
16. Because of increases in cost, some plants will have to shut down. Some industries that might be affected are beet sugar, dairies, electroplating, leather, meat packing, timber, and chemicals. The older and smaller firms are likely to be most affected.
17. No. Probably. See Ruff's paper in Mansfield, *Microeconomics: Selected Readings*.
18. See Ruff's paper in Mansfield, *Microeconomics: Selected Readings*.

Completion Questions

1. someone who makes no contribution to a public good, but who uses whatever amount of it that is provided.
2. public
3. benefit-cost
4. benefit-cost; one
5. marginal benefit; marginal benefit
6. Pecuniary
7. private; external
8. greater
9. greater
10. zero
11. effluent fee
12. Effluent fees

True or False

1. False 2. False 3. True 4. False 5. False 6. False 7. False 8. False 9. False 10. True
11. False 12. False.

Multiple Choice

1. *e* 2. *b* 3. *c* 4. *a* 5. *b* 6. *c* 7. *c*.